HOLIDAYS: This could be the year for that holiday you've always wanted. If there's somewhere you've always wanted to go then 1987 will see you realising your dreams. It might prove expensive but with all that lovely money coming your way . . .

FRIENDS: You have a strong will which sometimes puts your friends off. Although you're not, you can often appear big-headed which sometimes stops you making new pals. That's not to say you can't be a good friend and this year some of your mates will be looking for a shoulder to cry on — especially if they're Arians.

WORK/SCHOOL: Taureans tend to be slow learners so they need to put in a lot more work to achieve results. This is something you'll need to remember if you want to do well this year. It's all very well seeing your girly swot chums lying around doing nothing, but if you're going to keep up with them you'll need to get your act together.

HIGH POINTS: Your attractiveness to others is your best point and it will really come to the fore in 1987. Romance will figure highly and love will most definitely be in the air. That summer holiday of yours will find you with your head way up in the clouds but it's something you'll remember for a long time.

LOW POINTS: Work and school will be the low points of your year, and when you're down you'll be right down. When Taureans are in trouble they tend to reject offers of help and insist on getting out of a fix their own way. Go against the grain and be prepared to listen to what other people have to say.

GEMINI
MAY 21-JUNE 20

LOVE: You're the type of person who chops and changes her ideas, opinions . . . and boyfriends, quicker than most of us change our undies and 1987 won't be any different. There'll be lots of boys in and out of your life, but nothing serious — just the way you like it.

MONEY: The trouble with money is, the more you get, the more things you'd like to spend it on. Try saving up for a special blow-out rather than frittering it away on things you don't really need, then regret it later on.

HOLIDAYS: Geminians are supposed to be ''born travellers''. It's the chance to meet new people and go to new places that you enjoy, so whether you're going to Bognor or Bermuda you should have a great time and no doubt have lots of holiday romances!

FRIENDS: Although you love meeting new people, try to keep in touch with your old friends and don't desert them too much. Friendship's a two-way street — you've got to give as well as take.

WORK/SCHOOL: Geminians are notorious for getting bored, so make sure you've got a lot to keep you busy. However, don't go too far the other way and take on too many things that you can't finish. Take time and do a little planning, such as organising a sensible study

programme instead of having a mad panic the week before the exams!

HIGH POINTS: There's going to be lots of opportunities to do things and go places in '87 — particularly around July. All it needs is a bit of guts and the determination to see things through. Go for it.

LOW POINTS: You may have lots of opportunities coming your way; the only problem is, you're going to have to make decisions. Try not to lose too much sleep chopping and changing your mind about something and when you finally do decide to do something, wish you hadn't. You don't regret the things you *have* done, only the things you *haven't*.

CANCER
JUNE 21-JULY 21

LOVE: The year might start slowly, but you're not the type to be on your own for long. Relationships are best kept light and friendly, though — don't give your heart too easily, because you'll be the one to get hurt. Love may not be on the cards this year, but fun is. Lots of it.

MONEY: Remember money? That's the stuff grey-haired aunties used to give you so's you could buy lollipops and lucky bags, back in the mists of time. These days it's harder to come by, and harder still to hold on to — find out about Saturday jobs in your area and start stashing away the pennies. You don't need advice on how to spend it, though . . .

HOLIDAYS: You have a great sense of adventure, and a real knack for livening up the dullest of holidays. Your ideal holiday spot would be somewhere wild and romantic like Greece, Austria or Scotland, but even a weekend in a boarding house in Clacton-on-Sea wouldn't be the end of the world. Look at it with romance and spirit and you'll have just as much fun.

FRIENDS: One thing you're never short of is friends, because you're a good listener and you really do care about other people. You're loyal to your friends, but better still you're a good laugh to have around. If anything, though, you can be too trusting. Watch out for people taking advantage of your good nature!

WORK/SCHOOL: Work, for you, is something to be got through as quickly as possible so's you can get on with the real business of life. Try to give it a bit more attention, though. You can't always muddle through, and you might run into real trouble around May if you're not careful.

HIGH POINTS: The Summer's all set to be your best ever. You'll be full of energy and ideas and friends, male and female, will follow your lead. It might even be sunny!

LOW POINTS: Spring's the point where you're most likely to run into trouble this year — especially if you let your work get out of control. And once you're down, you're likely to stay down, feeling sorry for yourself and losing all that confidence. Keep plodding on, even through the dull bits, and you'll come out on top.

LEO
JULY 22-AUGUST 21

LOVE: As usual you'll seem to be in complete control of every situation. But just when you think you have organised the entire year ahead someone will turn up who you can't just boss around. You'll find him a challenge — someone a bit different.

Cont. on pages 94 and 95

£2.80

contents

Printed and Published in Great Britain by D. C. Thomson & Co., Ltd., 185 Fleet Street, London EC4A 2HS. © D. C. Thomson & Co., Ltd., 1987.

ISBN 0 85116 382 3

Starting together

So, at last the school hunk asks you out. Aside from being well over the moon, you begin to panic as to whether you'll actually get on. Will you have anything in common? Will you hate all the things he loves? He may be the sexiest thing since George Michael's belly button, but will you be sworn enemies by the end of the night???

Relax — we have the answer! Just try out the following on him . . .

"Em — excuse me big boy but before we go out on a proper date like, I wonder if you'd mind having a bash at this quiz. Although you're really hunky and all the rest of it — em . . . well we might not be suited to each other — know what I mean?

"So if you fill in your answers and put down what you think I would say for mine, then I'll do the same, when you've finished we'll compare them over some soft lights and soulful smoooocheronies. One point for each we get right, and the more points we get the better suited we are! Whaddya say matey?"

But how well would you get on?

YOUR QUESTIONS

1. Which one of the following would you have as a pet?
a. A Hamster
b. An Alsatian ✓
c. Neil Tennant.

2. Who's the hunkiest man alive? *Johnny*

3. Which one of the following do you find the most offensive?
a. Samantha Fox
b. Bernard Manning
c. Victoria Gillick. ✓

4. What do you take to bed with you?
a. A mug of hot chocolate and your Jackie annual. ✓
b. Your rollers and an overnight face pack.
c. Your teddy, who if you half close your eyes is the spitting image of Morten Harkett.

5. Are you good at Trivial Pursuit? *NO*

6. Would you know who Heather Haversham is?

7. Which one of these would get you legging it on to the dance floor?
a. Any Phil Collins smoocheroni ✓
c. James Brown's Living In America
d. The Smiths' Heaven Knows I'm A Pretty Miserable Fella Now.

8. Do you listen to Steve Wright In The Afternoon? *NO*

9. What would you rather see a boy in?
a. Faded denims and a cut off T-shirt
b. A duffle coat and cords
c. The skud.

10. Which one of these names appeal to you?
a. Rupert
b. Matt ✓
c. Charlie.

HIS QUESTIONS

1. What do you go for in a girl?
a. Big boobs ✓
b. Even bigger boobs
c. As long as she looks like Sammy Fox you're happy.

2. Which one of the following are you more like?
a. Wicksie
b. Ian Beale
c. Kelvin Carpenter

3. Would you do cooking at school? *Yes*

4. Would you wear ski-pants for men? *No*

5. What are Doctor Whites?
a. Em . . . well . . . something you'd rather not talk about
b. The doc' out of EastEnders.

c. Something that girls buy from the "personal hygiene" counter at Boots. ✓

6. How often do you go to the football? *None*

7. What do you wear in bed?
a. Setting gel
b. Stripey cotton pyjamas
c. Bed socks

8. If you were taking a girl somewhere special, where would you take her?

9. What's the job for you?
a. Editor of Jackie
b. Manager of Liverpool
c. Binman

10. Do you know who Matt Dillon is? *Yes*

0-7 Oh oh — I think we've made a beeg mistake here. Dump him now while you've got the chance. If you do go out with him don't come running to us for help!

8-14 Could be tricky. If he does take you out, take a list of harmless conversation starters like "Lovely weather we're having for this time of year etc." Steer well clear of storming in with "Don't ya think Samantha Fox and Patsy Kensit are the biggest dogs in the world?"

15-20 Ahh — you two were made for each other. For you not to go out with each other would be like Cagney without Lacey or Ethel without Willie. You've got it made and will probably stick together deeply in love for squillions of years. BORING!

TRIVIAL
Pursuits!

Try out our totally trivial pop test and find out how much you REALLY know about the charts.

1. Can you match up the following people with their respective girlfriends/boyfriends, husbands/wives?
a. Keith Chegwin
b. Paula Yates
c. Giovanna Cantone
d. Nik Kershaw
e. Leonie
f. Shirley Holliman
g. Jim Kerr

Bob Geldof
Chrissie Hynde
Tony Hadley
Martin Kemp
Roger Taylor
Maggie Philbin
Sheri

2. Which pop star has a fruit bat as a pet?

3. Sade's favourite holiday resort is,
a. Benidorm,
b. Ibiza,
c. Malta?

4. Which sort of college did Simon Le Bon attend before joining Duran Duran?

5. Boy George was expelled from school when he was 15. True or false?

6. See if you can match up the following pop stars with their birthdays!
a. Andrew Ridgeley   16th October
b. John Taylor   26th January
c. Tom Bailey   20th June
d. Gary Kemp   18th January

7. Nick Rhodes' most treasured possession is his,
a. cat,
b. video recorder,
c. camera?

8. What's Andy Ridgeley's brother called?

9. Nik Kershaw used to work in a dole office before becoming v. famous. True or false?

10. Can you remember the name of a-ha's first number one single?

11. Which D.J. banned Frankie Goes To Hollywood's "Relax" single?

12. How old was Bob Geldof when "Do They Know It's Christmas" was recorded?
a. Twenty-six
b. Thirty
c. Thirty-three

13. George Michael's real name is George Yogus. True or false?

14. See if you can match the following pop stars to his or her birthplace.
a. Annie Lennox   Luton
b. Paul Young   Newcastle
c. Alannah Currie   Glasgow
d. Midge Ure   Aberdeen
e. Sting   Auckland, New Zealand

15. Who are Peter Cox and Richard Drummie?

16. Roland from Tears For Fears' full name is Roland Orzabal De La Quintana. True or false?

17. From which films did these hits come?
a. "Living In America" — James Brown
b. "Let's Hear It For The Boy" — Denice Williams
c. "Eye Of The Tiger" — Survivor
d. "When Doves Cry" — Prince

18. I was born in Birmingham. I'm the bass player with two very successful bands. I spend most of my time in New York. My favourite drink is champagne. There are two other people with the same surname as myself in my main band. Who am I?

19. "Desperately Seeking Susan" starred which female megastar?

20. The following are all members of famous bands. Can you identify them?
a. Paul, Jim, Mick and Tony.
b. John, Gary, Tony, Steven, Martin.
c. Andy, Johnny, Mike, Stephen.

21. "Perfect Skin" was Lloyd Cole and the Commotions' first hit single. True or false?

22. Who is Jan Jones?

23. Morten Harket of a-ha used to work in,
a. a psychiatric hospital,
b. a baker's shop,
c. a tax office?

24. Can you match up the following groups with the record companies they record for?
a. Duran Duran   Parlophone
b. The Style Council   Polydor
c. The Eurythmics   RCA.

25. Before Go West hit the big time, all they could afford to eat was beans on toast, but what did they add to the meal?
a. Strawberry jam.
b. Garlic.
c. Sausages.

26. Nik Kershaw is under five feet tall. True or false?

27. Where did Wham! record their "Make It Big" album?
a. Germany.
b. New York.
c. France.

28. What is Madonna's middle name?

29. Which group did Paul King used to be in?
a. The Selector.
b. The Reluctant Stereotypes.
c. Haven't a clue . . .

30. Which magazine has the best pop features, pin-ups and Hot Gossip (that's a clue!) every week?

ANSWERS

The Reel Thing

CONTINUED ON PAGE 12

Get your hands on some boys' bits . . .

Shirt by Levi's. Hat from The Hat Shop, London; £9.75.

Shirt from branches of Gee 2; £19.99. Braces and sleevelets; £2.99 by Interface, available locally.

Hat available from most good sailing shops. Diamanté brooches from Top Shop.

ONE——OF

Denim Shirt by Levi's. Collar clips and bootlace tie by Interface, available locally.

Boxer shorts from Top Man, Marks and Spencer, and The Sock Shop. £2.99-£4.99.

Argyle socks available from The Sock Shop, or department stores.

—THE

Hat available from most good sailing shops; approx. £2.00. Brooches from Miss Selfridge. T-shirt is model's own.

BUT ON THE NIGHT . . .

THREE OF US, EH? WELL, I'M GLAD I CAME EARLY SO I CAN GET A GOOD SEAT! I CAN'T THINK WHERE EVERYONE'S GOT TO, PAULA!

I SUPPOSE I MIGHT AS WELL SHOW THE FILM. I HAVE TO PAY FOR IT ANYWAY.

WELL, PAULA, EDDIE'S IN THE PROJECTION ROOM. THERE'S JUST THE TWO OF US . . .

UNLESS YOU ESPECIALLY WANT A BLACK EYE, I'D ADVISE YOU TO WATCH THE FILM, RICK!

SO . .

"THE LANDLORD"

Woe is our heroine! Orphaned, destitute, penniless, and a villainous landlord due any moment to collect the rent!!

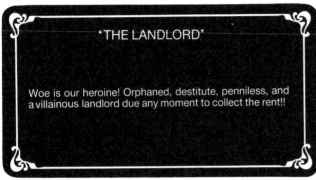

"Marry me, lass, and I'll let you off with the rent!"

"Marry you? Never! I'd rather take my chances with a rent tribunal!"

"If I can't have you, no-one shall!"

"Thank goodness for British Rail! The train will be late, I expect!"

In the nick of time, the hero arrives! (Sigh!) And with one blow lays low the villainous fiend!

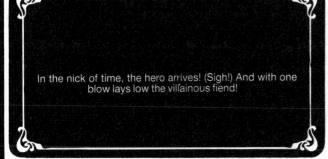

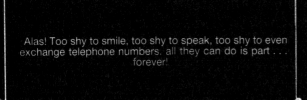

Alas! Too shy to smile, too shy to speak, too shy to even exchange telephone numbers. all they can do is part . . . forever!

WHAT A NICE FILM. EVEN RICK'S SNORING DIDN'T SPOIL IT. BUT THE ENDING NEARLY DID! TOO SHY TO GET TOGETHER? THEY MUST BE STUPID!!

AND I'VE BEEN STUPID, TOO! WHY SHOULDN'T I TELL EDDIE HOW MUCH I LIKE HIM? WHY SHOULDN'T I ASK HIM OUT? WHAT HARM CAN IT DO?

NO HARM AT ALL, PAULA! IN FACT, THE FILM MADE ME THINK THAT WAY, TOO! I WAS COMING TO SAY EXACTLY THE SAME THING TO YOU!

EDDIE! YOU WEREN'T MEANT TO HEAR! I MEAN . . .

OH, WHAT DOES IT MATTER? I'M GLAD YOU HEARD.

I'M GLAD, TOO, PAULA. I'VE WANTED TO ASK YOU OUT FOR A WHILE, BUT, WELL, YOU KNOW HOW IS IT . . . I SUPPOSE I'M JUST SHY.

HMMM! IS THAT STUPID FILM FINISHED YET, PAULA? HEY, PAULA?

I'M LOCKED IN! SOMEONE . . . ANYONE . . . HELP! LET ME OUT OF HERE! LET ME OUT! CAN ANYBODY HEAR ME?

SORRY, RICK, CAN'T HEAR A THING! AFTER ALL, ACTIONS SPEAK LOUDER THAN WORDS . . .

BAH!

THE END

HANDS UP!

● Give yourself a regular manicure . . .
1. Remove any old nail varnish, then use an emery board to shape your nails. Avoid a 'sawing' action — go from side t centre using long strokes.
2. Scrub gently with a nail brush to clean under your nails.
3. Use a cuticle remover to soften skin then gently push back cuticle with a cotto bud or an orange stick wrapped in cotto wool.
4. Apply hand cream and massage into hands and nails.

THINGS TO DO THIS SPRING

● Treat your hair to a special conditionin treatment and try a wash-in wash-out ha colour to liven it up after the dull winter months.

● Slough off any rough parts of skin with a well-soaped pumice stone or loofah. It' good for cleansing and gets your circulation going.

● Neaten up your eyebrows and pluck away any odd stragglers.

● Unearth the Immac and get rid of all that unwanted hair that's been making a comeback over winter. Legs will be on display soon and summer vest tops don't hide as much as layers of winter woollies!

● Lose a few extra pounds by eating slowly and having smaller portions. Munch raw vegtables and fruit instead of sweets. Drink lots of water — it'll take the edge off your appetite!

Blow away the winter cobwebs and spring into action . . .

WARDROBE WARFARE

Don't forget to attack your wardrobe as part of your spring clean routine! Here's a few of the things that should be heading for the bin . . .

Old underwear. Any ripped tights, bras that have gone more than a little off white, or knickers with extra-baggy elastic.

● Baggy jumpers. No, not the ultra trendy one you've just spent a fortune on but the few you've washed so much, they've gone totally out of shape! I mean, will you REALLY wear them again???

Anything you've kept from last year and STILL haven't worn! Chances are if you haven't sported any of the clothes yet, they'll probably still be lurking in your cupboard this time next year! Be ruthless, take them along to Oxfam. So what if they become fashionable in a few months' time . . . who wants to follow trends anyway!

Shoes beyond repair! Let's face it, there comes a time when it's not worth having shoes heeled yet again . . . Bin them and you've got an instant excuse for treating yourself to a new pair!

. . . And the things you should keep!

Old T-shirts. OK, so you may never wear them out on the town again, but they can always double up as a nightshirt or even to pop over your bikini on the way down to the beach in the summer!

Skirts. Let's face it, a skirt is always going to come in handy. Straight skirts NEVER go out of fashion whether you wear them down to the ground or chop them up into a tight-tight mini. Same goes for a gathered skirt — shorten it and you'll have a little number that'll never be out of place in your summer wardrobe! Or if it's the colour you've gone off, why not dye . . .

Sandals or pumps. These will always come in handy for the hols . . . even if you're just wearing them to paddle in. They're definitely worth having!

FACE SAVERS

LET OFF STEAM!

● Cleanse your skin, then cover your head with a towel and carefully lean over a bowl filled with boiling water.
Steam your face gently for about 10 minutes then pat your skin dry, splash with cold water, then dry again. Finish off by smoothing a little moisturiser into your skin.

RELAX!

● Put your hair back with a headband or scarf and cleanse, tone and moisturise your skin using gentle products. Rinse skin with luke-warm water, then apply a face mask.
While it's doing its job lie back and relax with two cold teabags or slices of cucumber over your eyes. You might not look very glamorous but it works wonders for tired eyes!
After the recommended time remove mask and gently pat your face dry with a soft towel, then apply a little moisturiser.

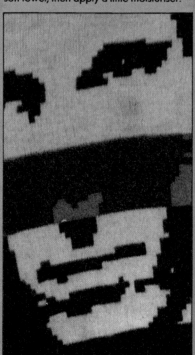

OUT AND ABOUT

● Spring has sprung so now's the time to get out and about and tackle everything you "just couldn't be bothered with" all through the winter . . .

● Start a new exercise routine to shed those pounds you've been hiding under those mega-baggy woollies! Join a local class (you'll find the addresses in the yellow pages) and then you'll HAVE to work out, or if you think you can force yourself, buy an exercise tape and bop around in your bedroom for a few hours every week. Of course you could always get someone to take you for a dance at the local disco . . .

● Get really into the Spring thing and take up a new sport. Running, swimming, cycling or tennis are all good fun sports which need little or no equipment (except for a bike, of course!) to start you off! Check with your local library for clubs in your area . . . who knows you may make some pretty interesting friends, too!

● Be energetic! Run round your room tidying up left right and centre! Get rid of all the junk that's been piling up under your bed or at the back of your wardrobe in one fell swoop. Be ruthless. OK, so you might think you just HAVE to keep that piece of paper that the sixth form hunk dropped out of his pocket on his way to Biology, but bin it — the more rubbish you get rid of, the more room you'll have to put new rubbish in . . .

● Prepare for the summer months by planning your new diet now. If you need to lose a few pounds, splash out on a calorie book and reduce your intake to around 1200 calories a day. (Remember to check with your doctor before beginning any diet). Even if you're quite happy with your shape, there's no excuse for not eating healthily — swop your white bread sarnies for wholemeal, spend your cash in the fruit market instead of the sweet shop and reach for the fresh fruit juice instead of yet another can of Coke . . .

The most famous blonde of them all.

B I
BOMBSHELL

Is it a myth, or do blondes *really* have more fun?

BELOUIS SOME:

● "I've tried all sorts of shades of blonde, I've also tried dying my hair other colours including black, but my favourite colour of all is white. I think the starkness of white hair has a lot more impact than a mere tone of blonde. Besides, when I start to go grey, nobody will even notice!"

MARILYN:

● "What *haven't* I done to my hair? I've had a full blonde Marilyn Monroe style, I've had it dark and I've had it medium honey-blonde, I've had pieces tied in and I've had bits cut off. Hair is the same as everything else in life — it gets spice from variety."

HOWARD JONES:

● "My natural hair colour is a sort of boring brown. I decided to change all that about five years ago, which was when I first started dying it. These days, I have a hairdresser who looks after it for me. The style and colour of my hair is always changing. A lot of people probably don't notice the changes, but you'll see the difference if you compare the way I look now to a photograph that was taken a couple of years ago. I don't think I'll be tempted to go back to boring brown again!"

o n d e

DIVINE:

● "I'm sorry to disappoint all my fans who think I'm the most gorgeous natural blonde they've ever seen — but, even though I may be gorgeous and I may be blonde, I have to admit that it sure ain't natural!

"In fact, underneath all that hair, I'm pretty nearly bald! I did think of having hair transplants but then I thought that would be silly. So I got myself plenty of wigs instead. This way I can be blonde one night, have black hair the next and be a red-head the night after."

SIMON LE BON:

● Good old Simon le Bon dyed his blonde locks black a year or so ago . . . then nearly drowned when his yacht sunk. Soon after he said goodbye to his single playboy image and tied the knot with Yasmin, so it's *obvious* blondes have more fun.

LIMAHL:

● "I've tried all sorts of things with my hair style. I was all black at one time and all blonde at another, and then I tried mixing black with blonde which is how I arrived at the streaked look.

"Bleached hair takes a lot of looking after, though, because it can get very dry and out-of-condition if you're not careful. I put baby oil on mine because ordinary hair gel makes it go frizzy."

KIM WILDE:

● "It was in my late teens that I finally decided to take the plunge and bleach my horrible mousey hair. I never regretted it either. I can honestly say that being a blonde made me feel much happier and more confident than I'd ever been before."

CATHY

▸ *(brunette)* I don't know about having more fun, but I certainly think there's lots of truth in the 'gentlemen prefer blondes' saying. I read somewhere that well over half the male population fancy women with blonde hair as opposed to any other colour. Seemingly they fancy blondes and go out with them for wild and exciting dates but end up taking brunettes home to Mummy and getting married to them.

Well, this is one brunette that'd prefer the wild and exciting dates . . .

SHIRLIE

▸ *(natural black hair)* Quite simply I don't think blondes have more fun. I have black hair and i have loads of fun.

TRACEY

▸ *(one of Jackie's fave. models)*·Course they do *(giggle)*. They get noticed more, don't they. *(more giggles)*.

NIKKI

▸ Well, yes! As you can see, this is me in Sri Lanka having fun with the boys *(it's like this all the time being a blonde!)*

JACKIE

▸ *(natural brunette)* No way! I can see why people believe blondes do have more fun — just listen to any joke involving a "good time girl", it always begins, "there was this big blonde . . ." Most of my friends have dark hair and if you've ever seen us out on the town together you wouldn't think "blondes have more fun" ever again — promise.

NATALIE

▸ *(natural dark brown hair)* No, of course blondes don't have more fun. And if you're wondering whether I'd rather look like Bet Lynch or Nastassia Kinski, I think the answer's obvious. But one thing's for sure — blondes THINK they're having more fun!

SHARON

▸ *(dyed blonde)* I have more fun now I'm a blonde — I might still be a bit of a mouse but at least I'm not described as "mousey". My boyfriend's got this thing about Samantha Fox but somehow I don't think it's just because she's a blonde . . .

LES

▸ *(mousey brown)* My wife's blonde — I guess the answer's — YES!

GOING BLONDE

If you want to go blonde, it's really best to go to a hairdresser's to get it done professionally, especially if your hair is naturally quite dark. Discuss which shade you'd like and whether you'd be best with all-over colour (with the problem of noticeable roots), highlights or tinted highlights (which are not so obvious as they don't involve bleach and fade out naturally).

If you are using home preparations, follow the instructions carefully.

Once you've gone blonde, condition well and get the ends trimmed regularly to avoid split ends.

If you're already blonde, a natural dye such as camomile or adding lemon juice to the final rinse will lighten the hair slightly.

According to a survey by Clairol, most men think blondes are sexy, bubbly and fun.

The reasons women give for going blonde are:
a. Those born blonde want to stay that way.
b. It makes them feel less dowdy.
c. They want a change.
d. They think it makes them more feminine.
e. It hides the grey.

ROOM FOR I[

Outgrown your dear little Donald Duck duvet? Fed up with that Noddy Wallpaper

The Twendy Room

OK, you've got your winklepickers and your mile-high haircut. If you reckon you're the twendiest girl in the street, better chuck out the floral winceyette bed linen and think up a new image . . .

● **The Basic room:** If you're lucky enough to have Noddy wallpaper, stick to it — if not, any old-fashioned wallpaper will do. The best floor covering is bright wacky lino — twendies have to suffer for their style — but otherwise a plain carpet in deep red, blue or green will do.

The Rug: If you're at all arty, get along to your local craft shop and look at the rug-making kits. Better still, design your own, using bright, clashing colours and wiggly patterns. What better way to while away the winter's evenings — you can always listen to The Jesus And Mary Chain at the same time!

● **The Basket Chair:** This may take some tracking down, but it'll be well worth it. Junk shops, jumble sales and flea markets are all worth searching, and ask everyone you know, too, as basket chairs lurk forgotten in attics throughout the land. A lick of fresh paint (choose bright yellow or red) and it'll be good as new.

● **The Lamp:** attics are packed with these, too — ikky, tasteless lamps with polka-dot shades and stands embedded with seashells or shaped like the Eiffel Tower. Get hold of the worst-looking one you can find, re-touch it with a little enamel paint if necessary, re-cover if the shade's tatty . . . and learn to love it.

● **The Dansette:** just the thing for those obscure albums in your obscure album collection. Dansettes can be picked up quite cheaply in junk shops — if you can't find one, though, try putting an ad. in a local shop window or newspaper. Dansettes aren't quite as advanced as your average hi-fi, and aren't really to be trusted with treasured records. If your records are the strange and whiny sort, however, Dansettes will make them better than ever . . .

● **The Tartan Blanket:** tartan is twendy. Hide your flowery duvet cover under a tartan blanket — if you can't find one in Tesco's, look in a motor-accessories shop for car blankets.

● **Decoration:** hunt through the junkshapes for 50's style magazines and record racks, and look out for old magazines and records to go in them. Splash out on a few James Dean posters for the walls and if you're still determined to cover up the wallpaper, hang a few 50's frocks or 60's minis on the walls. Pwetty twendy . . .

18

IPROVEMENT

...lear your room of sweet wrappers, odd socks and ancient bendy toys and start from scratch...

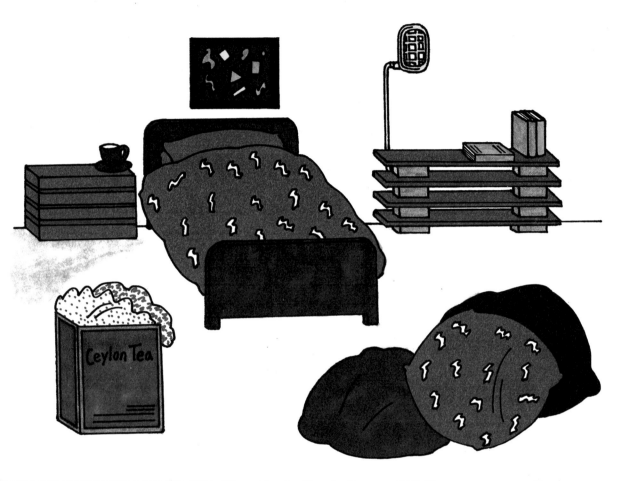

The High-Tech Room

If you're a modern girl, this is the [ro]om for you. It's stark, stylish, and dead [ch]eap to put together . . .

The Duvet Cover: you'll need 4½ [ya]rds of 54" wide fabric — choose strong [co]tton in deep red to match the [w]oodwork. Cut out two rectangles of [fa]bric 54" x 80". With the right side of the [fa]bric facing inwards, tack along three of [th]e edges to make a seam, leaving one [of] the 54" edges unjoined. Neatly turn [ba]ck a small hem on this unjoined edge. [M]achine or neatly stitch along the [se]ams, unpick the tacking and turn duvet [co]ver right side out. To keep the open [e]nd closed once the duvet's inside, [st]itch on 8 strong poppers along the [op]en side edge. Easy, eh? The fun bit is to [de]corate the duvet cover — spread a few [la]yers of newspaper inside the duvet [co]ver and paint on squiggly lines using [Ny]lon Color-Fun fabric paint. Once the [pa]int has dried, iron the duvet to set the [de]sign. Now turn the cover over and try [so]mething different on the other side . . .

● **The Bookshelf:** you need four small planks of wood, each painted with deep red gloss paint, and eight new (or, at least *clean*) housebricks. Stack the bricks and the planks, building-block style, to make a shelf. Dead easy — but don't overload it, or you might end up in the room below . . .

● **The Orange Box:** loiter around beside greengrocers' shops keeping an eye out for discarded fruit boxes — they're the sort with thin, slatted-wood sides. If you ask your greengrocer nicely, he'll probably give you one — take it home, dust it down and give it a coat of deep red gloss. Bedside tables have never been so cheap . . .

● **The Floor cushions:** look out for any remnants of strong cotton and use to cover spare pillows or cheap offcuts of foam. You can decorate these with squiggly lines, too!

● **The Garden Lamp:** if frilly table lamps just aren't your style, buy a high-tech garden or garage lamp from a department store or hardware shop. Ask a technical genius to see to the installation for you — unless you're an electronic whizz.

● **The Tea Chest:** tea chests are usually cheap or, better still, free — they're often advertised in the local press, but can be found lurking in attics. Ask around, and use them to store clothes, shoes etc., after removing any sharp metal bits.

The Romantic Room

The music's low, the lighting is dim — well, it has to be, doesn't it, to hide your sludge-green bedspread? If your room isn't quite the rose-tinted retreat of your dreams, now's the time to change it.

● **The basic room:** bully your dad to paint your room a fresh, stark white — or get permission to do it yourself! Enlist the help of a few mates, wear your oldest clothes, and move all the furniture and carpets out so you can't actually damage anything. Once the walls are dry, beg, borrow or bribe your way to a soft white or pale-pink carpet . . .

● **The Chest Of Drawers:** if your bedroom is ikky and brown, buy a large tub of white gloss paint and paint over the wood (first cover the surrounding area in thick layers of newspaper, or better still do the painting outside). Liven up the foot and headboard of your bed in the same way, if these are wooden — deep purple gloss looks really rich and decadent. Once the paint has dried thoroughly, add your own decorations in enamel paint. Hearts, flowers swirling lines and rainbow-curves all look good.

● **The Picture Frames:** look out in junk shops for el-cheapo picture frames and smarten them up with a lick of enamel paint. Hunt down your favourite magazine pictures and slushy snapshots and put 'em behind glass.

● **The Duvet Cover:** buy or make (see before) a plain, white duvet cover, and trim the edges with lace. Buy some cotton remnants in pinks and purples, together with a sheet of thin wadding from any good fabric store. Cut out a heart shape from cotton fabric, then a slightly smaller heart from the wadding. Tack the wadding to the wrong side of the fabric so there is a margin of about an inch of fabric showing around the outside of the wadding. Carefully turn in the margin of fabric and press neatly, so that the right side of the fabric shows a neat, cotton heart with a slightly padded look. Make several of these in various pastel shades, and arrange on the topside of your duvet cover. Attach the applique hearts with tiny, neat stitches around the edges of each heart, and unpick the tacking stitches to finish. If you get very adventurous, you can try big, swirly shapes too — or, if you can't get the hang of it at all, splash out on a few tubs of Dylon Color-Fun fabric paint and set to work with a brush instead.

● **The Cushion:** cut two large heartshapes from fabric remnants. With the fabric inside out, stitch a neat seam around the heart about 1″ from the edge, leaving a 2″ gap. Turn the fabric heart the right side out, stuff with Kapok and neatly stitch to close. For extra slush, sew a length of Broderie Anglaise or lace around the edge.

● **The Screen** — search through the local junk shops for an old, folding screen — or, better still, bribe a technical genius to help you make one. They're great for dressing and undressing movie star style, as well as hiding ikky corners of the room. Decorate the screen. yourself with a bold painted design or soft drapes of muslin or lace.

● **The Plants:** plants are easy. You don't have to make them, just nip down to Tesco's and buy in a couple of spider plants. You can grow more spiders by placing the little baby-spiders that sprout from the big plant into little pots of moist soil. Don't cut the baby spiders off from the mother plant until you're sure they've taken root.

● **Decoration:** hide yukky bits of furniture under offcuts of crushed velvet drape lace here and there and store all your excess woolly hats and thermals in tasteful wickerwork baskets. Ahh . . .

We fire 20 questions at Paul King

ARE YOU BIG HEADED?
I'm self-confident, but I don't really get a chance to be big-headed because the rest of the band have even bigger egos than I have! Honest!

WHAT WAS THE HAPPIEST MOMENT OF YOUR LIFE?
Joining King, getting on "Top Of The Pops" . . . whatever happens to me tomorrow, who can tell?

DID YOU ENJOY YOUR CHILDHOOD?
It was good and bad, like everybody else's. But I grew up very quickly so I didn't have the time to get bored with childhood . . .

WHO IS THE MOST FAMOUS PERSON YOU'VE EVER MET?
Terry Wogan. Well, he's on telly the most, anyway!

WHICH IS YOUR FAVOURITE POP RECORD?
"Love's Gonna Let Me Down" by Toots and The Maytals. It's brilliant!

WHICH IS YOUR MOST HATED POP RECORD?
"Shaddup Your Face" by Joe Dolce. I think if there was a poll to find out everyone's worst ever record, this would win hands down. Does anyone like it?

WHAT IS YOUR FAVOURITE COLOUR?
Anything that clashes!

QUESTION TIME WITH...

PAUL KING

IF YOU COULD CHANGE ONE THING ABOUT YOUR APPEARANCE, WHAT WOULD IT BE?
I've changed so many things about my appearance, I wonder whether there's anything left? I'm quite happy at the moment, though.

DO YOU COLOUR YOUR HAIR?
Not as much as I used to. Why . . .? Do you think a blue rinse would suit me? It's naturally dark.

HAVE YOU EVER HIT ANYBODY?
Oh yes. I'm not aggressive by nature, but when I do get angry, I can be quite violent.

IF YOU WEREN'T A POP STAR, WHAT WOULD YOU LIKE TO DO?
I'd like to be either an ice-skater or an archaeologist. Or, better still, an ice-skating archaeologist. There's not a lot of them around, you know!

HAVE YOU GOT A FAVOURITE FOOD?
Tuna and mayonnaise, especially on sarnies!

CAN YOU STAND ON YOUR HEAD?
I don't intend to try! I probably could, though.

DO YOU LIKE DRESSING UP?
If there's a choice between dressing *up* and dressing *down*, then I will certainly choose the first one. It's the sensible thing to do, surely!

WHERE DO YOU GET YOUR STYLE?
It's a total mixture and it changes a lot. The original King style came from a cartoon of Jimminy Cricket. But I take ideas from all over the place and put them together in unusual combinations. You either love it or loathe it.

WHAT IS YOUR HOBBY?
Being a pop star!

WHAT'S THE FIRST THING YOU DO IN THE MORNING?
Yawn. Doesn't everyone?

WHAT'S THE LAST THING YOU DO AT NIGHT?
Yawn.

WHAT WILL YOU BE DOING WHEN YOU ARE 65?
My master plan doesn't stretch that far into the future. I'm still working on my plans for the next year or two. Once I've got that sorted out, I'll start to worry about later on in life.

ANY SPECIAL MESSAGE . . .?
Take the bad with the good, the bitter with the sweet, and let life take care of itself!

A BIT OF cultu

THE STEVE

Wears: Whatever his mum lays out for him that morning or, failing that, anything that comes to hand, as long as it's practical and guaranteed not to cause offence.

Hair: Generally just left to grow between three-monthly haircuts. For a special occasion a Steve will comb it into a middle parting and secure it with the Brut hairspray the girl next door got him for Christmas.

Likes: Grown-up comics like the Beano and 2000 AD.
Steve Wright In The Afternoon.
Thinking about girls with big boobs and blonde hair.
Dire Straits and other bands that can play their instruments.

Dislikes: Buying clothes.
Girls who try to chat him up.
His mum throwing out his collection of Beanos.

THE PSYCHOBILLY

Wears: Baseball jackets, jeans that are too short, Cramps T-shirts, bowling shirts and creepers. When their flat-tops begin to look a bit limp, the psychobilly always keeps his 'Benny' hat ready to whip out at the right moment.

Hair: For girls it's Doris Day or bust, and as for the lads, as long as it's flat on top and sticks out a bit in front then you're all right. Like the punks, they're firm believers in Boots' hairspray.

Likes: The Meteors, the Cramps and any bands with Cat in their names.
Boxer shorts with outrageous patterns.
Stompin' (hitting each other with their elbows and punching their hands in the air).

Dislikes: People who say Elvis was fat.
People who say James Dean couldn't drive.
People who say that flat-tops look like shoe brushes turned hair side up.

THE TRENDIES

Wears: Anything second-hand, especially if it comes from Flip or shops like that. Even in the days of British Summertime, the trendies can be found sweating under their trendy macs. They're *so* fond of fifties anoraks and frocks and are prone to carrying their original copies of 'Absolute Beginners' around in duffel bags and fifties handbags.

Hair: The golden rule here is, if it looks as though it's been cut by a blind man with a pudding bowl then it's all right! Trendy boys are also prone to dipping into a tub of Brylcreem now and then.

Likes: Echo and the Bunnymen and anyone else who comes from Liverpool!
Drinking hot chocolate ('cos you can't get cappuccino in Tesco's).
Mean and moody film stars like James Dean and Rupert Everett.
Alternative comedy shows and poets(!) like John Cooper Clarke.

Dislikes: Buying clothes from Top Shop.
Anything that looks new and modern.
Meat and nuclear bombs.
Bands like a-ha and Duran Duran.

re

JACKIE LOOKS AT WHICH CULT IS WHICH . . .

THE PUNK

Wears: Anything that can be torn apart and sprayed with 'Anarchy' on the back of it. Also fond of stripey jumpers and trousers and claims to have been wearing crosses and chains while Madonna was still cleaning the toilets in New York nightclubs.

Hair: Sponsored by Boots' Firm Hold. Most punks have bleached, shaved and sprayed their hair so many times chances are they won't have any left by the time they're 25.

Likes: Bands like Bauhaus who wear lots of black clothes.
Getting their jeans as dirty as possible.
Mary from EastEnders before she became wet.
Crazy Colour.

Dislikes: Watching TV (Yup — even Brookside).
Bands like the Cult-punks turned Hippies.
Work!
Rain — 'cos it makes their haircuts flop.

THE CASUAL

Wears: Tracksuits, tennis shirts and anything with Italian names. The Casual's main guide when buying clothes is that if 20,000 other people in town are wearing it then it must be OK.

Hair: Falls into two schools: The Paul Weller, let it hang over your eyes job or the Charlie Nicholas, permed at the back and long on top style.

Likes: The Minds (Simple), The Council (Style), & Spear (Of Destiny).
Trying to grow a moustache.
Trying to get girls drunk at parties.
Getting into Barney Rubble (trouble) at football matches.

Dislikes: Girls who don't come up with the goods.
Boys who aren't hard.
Reading pages of the paper other than the sports section.
Going to visit their grandma.

Relax

When the going gets tough, the tough get going — but some of us just turn into quivering wrecks . . .

Are you one of those people who lurch from one crisis to another and can never seem to relax? Does the mere thought of a big date/an exam/the fact you've just lost the family dog/broken mum's best china and know you'll have to own up soon make you break into a cold sweat, ready to climb onto the window ledge and jump? Well stop panicking, help is on its way.

For a start panicking isn't going to help with the date/exam/finding the dog etc. Maybe nothing can help, maybe you'll get excommunicated from the family and told never to darken the doorstep again but if it happens, it happens, panicking won't change the outcome in the slightest.

Being calm comes naturally to some. Most of us, though, have to work at it.

There's lots of natural preparations which are supposed to calm you down such as **aromatherapy oils** *(around £2 from The Body Shop)*
Try:
Lavender — bath then massage your neck and shoulders with the oil.

Chamomile — inhale and massage onto head.

Neroli — massage throat and face.
Or how about sipping a soothing cup of **chamomile tea?**

If you're always in a panic about one thing or another, it might be worth enrolling in a **yoga** class to try to improve your 'inner serenity' as well as your figure. Lots of people try a sort of self hypnosis trick too — lying perfectly still and concentrating on nothing.

A lovely long soak in a **warm bath** with some nice bath oil or bubbles can work wonders also.

It's often worth sitting down with a sheet of paper and working out what could be the worst possible outcomes and whether in fact you're just making a mountain out of a molehill. Being able to sit down and think clearly about something always helps to get things into their correct perspective.

JACKIE I don't panic much, but I do tend to worry about things so I've worked out my own way of calming myself down. Say I'm worried about going on a first date or something. I just think of something I've achieved or I'm proud of and I think well, if I've done *that* I can handle anything.

NATALIE I'm a great believer in chamomile tea — works every time. If it's good weather I often go off and cycle for miles — by the time I get back home I'm too whacked to start panicking about anything.

CATHY Sounds wet, but I find if you borrow a friendly shoulder it helps.
I broke up with a boyfriend at the same time a mate from school broke up with his girlfriend. We met, got talking and ended up crying on each other's shoulders — literally.
Now if there's ever anything worrying or upsetting either of us we just phone each other up and have a good moan. He's great, especially if I'm having boyfriend trouble because he can often help you understand why the chap in question did what he did (being a chap himself) and is always ready with a cuddle to make you feel better.
If he's not around, my teddy bear's a good substitute.

MIKE When I start panicking I go and *do* something — anything — to take my mind off whatever the problem happens to be. It doesn't solve the problem but at least you can forget it for a while.

JEAN I usually take the dog for a walk — that usually calms me down. If I'm angry or upset I always feel better if I throw something (preferably at the person I'm annoyed with).

SHEENA I never stop myself panicking. I have a two minute complete panic and then I'm calm and can cope with anything. The ONLY thing which stops me panicking is if someone else does it. Two panicking people is just too much.

LIPSTICK POWDER & PAINT!

Make it a date to remember with our step-by-step guide to looking good . . .

HAIR WE GO

25

Have a quick shower or a warm bath — not too hot, otherwise you'll just get all hot and bothered! Remember to de-fuzz underarms and legs and dust yourself lightly with talc — choose one to match your perfume if possible.

 Shampoo and condition your hair and tie it back or wrap it in a towel out of the way.

 Don't go near your make-up bag until you've cleansed, toned and moisturised your skin. Give the moisturiser a chance to sink in while you lay out what you're going to wear and do any last-minute ironing.

BLUSH BABY

Now you can apply your make-up.
Dot a little foundation over your face and throat, then blend in well using your fingertips or a damp cosmetic sponge. Use a concealer stick to cover up any spots and blemishes or dark circles under your eyes. Blend in well.

Apply a light dusting of translucent face powder then stroke on a little powder blusher, using a soft brush.

Now concentrate on the eyes, keeping in mind what clothes you're going to be wearing. Give your lashes a couple of coats of mascara, letting the first coat dry before you apply the second.

Outline your lips with a lip pencil, then fill in using a lipstick or lip brush. Blot with a tissue to 'set' the lipstick.

Finally, check for any stray bits of mascara or make-up and remove with a cotton bud.

WAVE YOUR WAND

 By this time your hair should be practically dry so give it a quick spray of water (use a plant sprayer!) and dry and style in the normal way.

 Get dressed and give yourself a quick spray of perfume. Double-check everything in the mirror — and you're all set!

 The doorbell rings. Have a great time!

READY, STEADY, BLOW

It's his funny little

habits that endear you to

him . . . or is it? Compare

the boy in your life to the

two here and see if you've

come up with a right Wally

or a proper Charlie!

WALLY

WALLY . . .

. . . calls you 'pet'
. . . reads books about TV repair on the bus
. . . copies diagrams of electrical circuits in hi-fi shops
. . . has to be reminded about cleaning under his fingernails
. . . wears his dad's cardigans
. . . never notices that you've had your hair done
. . . has a hairstyle which makes him look like he just got out of bed
. . . pulls on the first thing he finds in the morning
. . . won't go to discos because he'd rather stay in and play with his Scalextric
. . . won't use anything to get rid of his spots
. . . wears his socks for anything up to a week at a time
. . . prefers trousers with a slight flare
. . . refuses to buy singles 'because they're only for teenyboppers'
. . . did two weeks of a psychology course and thinks he knows it all
. . . votes for Bamber Gascoyne in student elections
. . . harbours a secret ambition to be president of the students union
. . . uses Sigue Sigue Sputnik as proof that the music industry is going to the dogs
. . . has a bedroom wall covered in Genesis posters
. . . pretends to play guitar to Eric Clapton records
. . . drinks one pint of lager and is ill for three days
. . . has a pie on a roll and two cans of Coke for lunch.
. . . thinks it's really important to be 'socially aware'

CHARLIE . . .

. . . forgets your name and calls you by one of his ex-girlfriends' instead
. . . can't hear a word you're saying because he's always plugged into his Walkman
. . . points out that you've got another spot and keeps count
. . . wears your new clothes
. . . won't let you touch his hair because it's solid with gel
. . . takes three hours to get ready to go out
. . . won't step out of the house for a pint of milk unless his outfit co-ordinates
. . . wears clothes he can't actually walk in
. . . can't see a thing at discos but refuses to take his sunglasses off
. . . thinks he's going to be a pop star because his parents bought him a guitar he can't play
. . . cultivates a slight American accent in preparation for being famous
. . . likes cult bands until they get a single in the Network charts and everyone else likes them too
. . . covers his walls in pics of Madonna and Marilyn Monroe and compares you unfavourably
. . . name drops pop stars because he once got their autographs
. . . constantly refers to the time he got his photo in a fanzine
. . . is too cool to talk to your friends
. . . doesn't give you a chance to look in the mirror because he's too busy admiring himself
. . . only dances to indie records
. . . uses up the last of your hairspray
. . . thinks every girl he meets is in love with him

" d i r e t

CHARLIE

raits"

WH

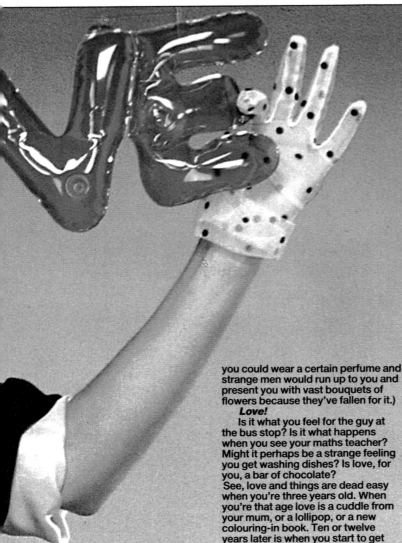

It's in the dictionary between *Louvre Doors* and *Low* and causes huge problems . . .

Love!

People write more songs about it than anything else. It's probably the most powerful emotion anyone can experience. It pulls people together and pushes them apart. It makes them happier than anything else and it makes them more sad than anything else will. It makes people do the strangest things. (If we believed what they say in adverts,

you could wear a certain perfume and strange men would run up to you and present you with vast bouquets of flowers because they've fallen for it.)

Love!

Is it what you feel for the guy at the bus stop? Is it what happens when you see your maths teacher? Might it perhaps be a strange feeling you get washing dishes? Is love, for you, a bar of chocolate?

See, love and things are dead easy when you're three years old. When you're that age love is a cuddle from your mum, or a lollipop, or a new colouring-in book. Ten or twelve years later is when you start to get into the big league, and from there on it becomes one of the biggest motivating forces behind what you do (incidentally, it also becomes one of the biggest problems you'll ever have!)

So how do you define it? Because one of the biggest headaches is going to be trying to work out exactly what it *is!* Not perhaps as silly as it may sound — after all, it's a word that everyone uses but nobody really tries to explain. Look up the dictionary and what does it say? Nothing really, even it cops out a bit when, in between Louvre Doors and Low, it rambles on about affection, reverential regard (their phrase, not ours) and devoted attachment. The reason's because, just as we could go on for page after page on what love means to everyone in the Jackie office it means different things to different people. It's just entirely personal.

Anyway, it's a lot easier to use the word 'love' in songs rather than trying to fit in a phrase like 'mutual respect and affection' which is rather difficult to rhyme with anything.

Possibly the biggest mistake anyone makes is to confuse love with appearance. Just because a certain sixth-former has really cute dimples when he smiles doesn't mean that he's going to treasure your company. Cue the ancient ABC song:

"If you judge a book by the cover then you judge the look by the lover."

One car, after all, doesn't go faster than another *simply* because it's got a sun-roof and a fancy gear knob.

As a general rule, love (in the more successful cases) is based on emotional needs. It doesn't really have that much to do with boxes of chocolate, candlelit dinners or even soft-focus ads for Cadbury's Flake. It's to do with liking someone, them liking you, being able to put up with each other's annoying habits, having sympathy with each other . . . see, there we go again, trying to define this (crazy little) thing!

Everybody has an idea about who their perfect boy/girl/blob from outer space would be. In many cases it's someone who can help them be things they're not, and/or will complement what they can do, like a team. For example, if you're shy, then it'll be someone who is popular and will help you meet people. If you can't bring yourself to make decisions, then it'll be someone who is decisive.

Sounds quite simple, doesn't it? Of course, it's not. If it was, then we could all join a computer dating agency and find entirely compatible 'partners'. Mary Smith, who can't bear to be told what to do would meet Tommy Jones, who is happiest being told what to do. And together they'd live happily ever after.

But as we say, it's just not that straightforward. Everyone changes to suit the situation they find themselves in. No-one is predictable all of the time.

Confused yet? It's a difficult subject!

In fact it's such a huge subject, with such enormous implications, that there can be no hard and fast rules, no hand-book to tell you what to do next . . . so this is where you stop reading and go and find out!

Hair by Allan Soh.

double take

AFTERSHAVE

Most aftershaves contain astringent which dries the skin slightly — ideal for boys with normal to oily skin.

It's also an enemy of spots. Just dab a little on with cotton wool and you should feel it drying out the little devils!

PERFUME

No, we're not suggesting your boyfriend wears the same perfume as you — just that he applies his aftershave in the same way!

Perfumed aftershaves tend to sting the skin after shaving so he should splash them around the neck and chest and on elbow grooves and wrists instead of over his face like Henry Cooper!

MOISTURISER

For blokes with normal to dry skin most ranges now do a "shave balm" which is what we would call a moisturiser! No wonder boys are such big softies.

DEPILATORY

A depilatory (hair removing cream) isn't just for girls — blokes can now be smoothies, too! Carson Magic Cream Shave is specially designed to gently dissolve facial hair preventing those annoying "razor bumps" — makes kissing him much nicer, too!

SHAVING BRUSH!

His big, soft shaving brush is an ideal way to exfoliate your skin. Just lather your face with a gentle soap and water or a facial wash and gently rotate the brush. It should leave your skin feeling healthy and glowing.

Some skin care experts believe that the reason why male skins tend to get lines less rapidly around the mouth and cheeks is because daily shaving acts as a natural exfoliant.

We'll be borrowing their razors next!

HAIR CARE

Blokes no longer have any excuse for going about with greasy "John Travolta" hair. Unless they're trendy Brylcreem boys, they should be taking as much care of their hair as you do.

Henara do a range of Henna products especially for men including hair styling gel and a scalp treatment wax so they've no excuse!

And next time you're off to the hairdresser's drag your fella along too. Tell him getting a short back 'n' sides at the barber's isn't hip!

"Pig In The Middle"

Who said pork chops? Away and pig on someone your own size . . .

"You **pig!**"

How many times has someone called you that? It's one of the many insults that's flung around the **Jackie** office. Ha! But what they don't realise (and keep this to yourself) is that being called a pig isn't really an insult after all. It's **actually** a compliment.

I mean, why is it we see comparisons with pigs as unfavourable? The pig is a loving, lovely, **lovable** creature who can come out of the sty and make your house beautiful.

There is a line of argument that we are decended from the pig. Take that Great British pastime of sunbathing, for example. It is a popular misconception that pigs like rolling in mud. Nonsense! They actually like sunbathing and lie on their backs to have their tummies sunned — that's the truth.

So, let's open the door and see how we can let pigs brighten our home. Fans of Coronation Street will be aware of Hilda Ogden's living room decor – her ghastly mural (or "muriel" as Hilda would say) and hideous flying bird wall plaques. She obviously knows nothing about interior design. The room would be given much greater ambience if she replaced those stupid birds with flying pigs.

Has your mum ever looked at your bedroom and said "This place is like a pig sty"? This is no insult! A Pig Sty is, as a matter of course, messy — but they are only made that way by all the things that humans throw into them. If the pigs had their way they'd be very tidy. Take the little pig on this page, for example, look how it keeps my desk tidy.

Piggy banks are just lovely, too! A smiling little pig face with a chubby body decorated in floral patterns can brighten up any day, not to mention a dark corner. There are so many different kinds of piggy banks that it would be easy — and very cheap — to start a collection. Your own little herd, you might say, er . . . or should that be flock?

Pigs are great friends and that cleverest of all little bears, Winnie The Pooh, certainly knew that. His constant companion, Piglet, brightened his playtime hours and a little padded replica of Piglet is a great playtime companion for children (up to the age of 60). Piglet is a bit of a looker too, a far better decoration for your dressing table than a picture of George Michael.

If you're game for a bit of fun, pigs can come to your rescue there, too. No I don't mean in the play pork, or the amusement pork. What about Pass The Pigs?

So, the next time anybody tells you that you're acting the pig, think of all the little beauties . . . and the smile on your face will puzzle the person trying to give you abuse, and paying you a compliment!

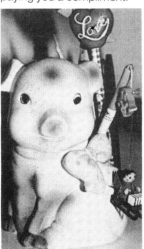

Your very last plassy carrier has exploded all over the classroom, showering one and all with furry boiled sweets and homework jotters. You really need something a little more durable — like a pwetty twendy hatbox handbag or a polka-dot duffel bag, for instance . . .

WORK SHOP IN THE BAG!

HATBOX HANDBAG

1. First catch your hatbox — small, round vinyl-covered vanity cases can be found cheaply in toy shops, jumble sales or junk shops.
2. Re-line the bag — rip out the ikky nylon lining and choose a new lining from paisley, polka-dot or tartan remnants.
3. Trace out the shape of the box-lid on to paper, then cut out two pieces of cloth a little larger than the pattern. Turning in the raw edges as you go, glue one piece inside the lid and one into the bottom of the bag.
4. Cut a broad strip of cloth to fit around the inside wall of the case and glue into place neatly, folding down the raw edges as you go for a neat finish.
5. If you want to alter the colour of the vanity-case, paint with shoe dye — or, for a really glossy look, black enamel paint. Varnish to protect.

DUFFEL BAG

1. Draw a circle (radius 4″) on to a piece of strong cardboard and cut out. Now cut a circle of strong fabric slightly larger than the cardboard pattern.
2. Cut a rectangle of polka-dot fabric 16″ x 14″. With the fabric inside out, join together the 16″ edges to make a tube shape.
3. With the fabric tube and the fabric circle inside out, join together to make a duffel bag shape. Turn right-side out to hide raw edges and seams. Place the cardboard circle inside the bag for extra strength.
4. Turn a neat hem along the top edge of the duffel bag. Now cut a strip of contrasting fabric, 14″ x 5″ and hem the two 5″ edges neatly. With the fabric inside out, join the two 14″ edges in a neat seam. Turn right-side out.
5. Pin the contrasting tube to the top of the duffel bag, along the inside edge. Stitch neatly to join. Don't stitch the open ends of the casing together!
6. Take a length of card 1½ metres long, thread through the casing and knot the ends together.

3 steps

The chasing, the catching and the ones that get away . . . we take you through the 3 stages of a relationship!

THE CHASE IS ON!

Meeting and pursuing is often the best and most exciting part of a relationship, especially if it's a real Mills & Boon sweep-you-off-your-feet type start. Like when Debbie met Tony: "We met at the restaurant where Tony works. I went there a lot with my parents and I used to flirt with Tony. He was so handsome and charming and on our third visit he slipped me a note on my dessert dish asking me out. It was *so* romantic — like in a book! When we went out together for the first time he was wonderful, he seemed to know just how to treat a girl.

"My Mum and Dad didn't know I was seeing him — Dad would've gone berserk — and that element of intrigue just made it more exciting and romantic."

In a romance like this, to start, there are absolutely no doubts. It's all so terrific — this boy is *the* one.

And there's the boy you've fancied for ages who you finally *do* go out with. Heaven, as Rebecca found out. "Of course I fancied Martin — all the girls did! He was real hero material, tall and sexy, captain of the football team. Martin's brother was in my class and it was at Rob's birthday party I met him properly. He asked me to dance and later he asked me out — I was over the moon. He could've taken me anywhere and I'd have thought it was terrific."

Of course it doesn't always happen quite so romantically. Sometimes there's an initial doubt, a reluctance and the one who *is* keen has to be a bit more persuasive and chase a little harder. Jenny for instance wasn't too sure about

going out with Sean. "Although I thought he was a bit of a show-off I was flattered by the attention he paid to me. He was just determined to go out with me, and wouldn't take no for an answer!"

Sometimes the doubts are much bigger. Sometimes you go out with someone you don't even like! Sounds crazy? Well, how about Claire? "Everyone knew Chris really fancied me and they all thought it was dead funny. Poor Chris is what you might call a wimp, at least to look at. It was quite a joke the way he used to hang around me. I went out with him once, because I felt sorry for him and because my mates put me up to it. For a laugh. But once I'd been out with him it was different because he wasn't like other boys, he was thoughtful and interesting and I got to really like him."

GETTING TO KNOW YOU!

Once you've met the object of your desire the next bit is the getting-to-know-you stage. It's when you discover each other's irritating little habits. Like the way he hums along with his personal hi-fi when you can't hear the tune or how he cleans his ears out with his hankie. Sometimes however, you're so head-over-heels, nose-over-toes in love that you can't see anything wrong with him at all. Back to Rebecca: "Martin and I seemed perfect. The more I got to know him the more I liked him. He was good-looking, and had a terrific sense of humour. He took me home to meet his family and they were great too. I fitted in well and they welcomed me.

"After a month or two I was having these rings-and-bells-type fantasies about Martin and me. It was about then I noticed that Martin was cooler about the whole thing.

"I'd always assumed that he thought it was as perfect as I did, but he noticeably cooled off."

Let's face it, everyone has faults, but with your boyfriend you're probably quite prepared to gloss over it, like

Debbie was. "Tony was, in the nicest possible way, dead bossy. He decided where we'd go on dates, what we'd eat, he even told me what to wear! At first it was sort of sexy and 'macho', but after a while it really got on my nerves."

Jenny took a while to make up her mind about Sean. "Going out with Sean was fun at first. He and his friends got up to the most amazing tricks and at first I joined in. Then I started to get fed-up. The 'larks' (which were Sean's main interest) seemed really stupid and childish and Sean's continual showing-off got on my nerves. We rowed a lot but we always seemed to make it up in an equally dramatic way."

Claire, who you remember went out with Chris for what seemed like the wrong reasons found that, once she got to know him well, he was nice. "Once I

to heaven?

got to know Chris, like I said, I really got to like him. Trouble was it was only *me* who thought so. All my mates thought he was a right wally. Chris didn't like doing things with my friends and usually wanted us to be by ourselves."

ENDING UP . . .

Pretty soon it becomes clear which relationships are going to last a bit longer and which aren't. Sometimes the end happens like World War Three! Just like Jenny and Sean. "The crunch came when I found out he had another girl. On the nights he told me he was at football practice he was seeing someone else. Then one night I went down the disco and there he was with this silly girl hanging round his neck drooling all over him. I lost my temper and we had a

blazing row, right there in the disco. I stormed out and ever since I've totally ignored him."

In Rebecca's case too there was a confrontation but the outcome wasn't quite what she'd hoped for. "I felt I couldn't win. I could see us drifting apart but it seemed whatever I did I'd lose. I finally decided to confront Martin over his coolness and he accused me of being too serious and of course he was right. He explained — and he was so calm and reasonable I felt like hitting him — that he just didn't want to be serious yet with anyone. He suggested that we just stay friends — I had to agree."

Tony and Debbie didn't actually row either but the little irritations became large obstacles and they finally realised they just weren't compatible. "Finally I got fed-up with Tony telling me what to

do and he got fed-up with me being, as he put it 'awkward', that is standing up to him.

"Our backgrounds were too different, we didn't fit in with each other's family and friends and our relationship wasn't deep enough to take that."

Incompatibility, just not getting on or not liking each other enough, is probably the biggest reason for break-ups. In the end Claire, like Debbie, ditched the unfamiliar for the familiar. "I finally broke up with Chris when I decided to go out with another boy, but Chris was getting fed-up too because of my loyalty to my mates. I liked Chris a lot but I needed my friends more. And once I actually went out with the other boy I didn't like him very much, but that's the way it is, isn't it?"

ONE of the greatest things about summer is that it's a brilliant time to fall in love! But it's also a very dangerous time, particularly if you're on holiday, in a different environment, and more relaxed about life generally.

Holiday romances can be a wonderful boost to your ego. They can make you feel like a million dollars, but unless you're very, very sensible, or very, very careful, they can also break your heart.

When you're away, particularly in a place where you don't know anybody except maybe your immediate family or mates, somebody apparently taking a serious interest in you can make you sigh with relief!

Suddenly you've someone to talk to and go out with. And if that someone *also* just happens to be a pwetty hunky lad, it's an added bonus!

The trouble is, it's all too easy to believe you're really in love when he kisses you tenderly on the beach in the moonlight instead of your usual snog up the close with the guy from the local chippy!

Sometimes you really may fall in love. Something that starts off as just a brief meeting may mature and actually grow into something that keeps you together for months, or even years. But the chances of it happening do, honestly, tend to be on the slim side.

For a start, unless it's a one-in-a-million fluke, you'll both come from different towns which are, in all probability, miles apart. So when you're both back home

36

mmer lovin'

again with all your mates in familiar surroundings, the sheer practicalities of meeting up often enough or talking to each other often enough may very well knock what 'romance' there was on the head. Gradually, simply because you *don't* see each other, you'll begin to drift apart in your feelings.

Independently you'll both get involved with other people, because these people are *there*, close to you.

The phone calls'll get less frequent, and instead of writing to each other every day, it'll become every other day, then maybe twice a week — and finally the letters will just stop.

Provided that *is* the way it happens, and provided neither of you is badly hurt, then nothing's lost.

But if one of you wants to keep the relationship going and the other doesn't, life can get very messy because the one who's still writing or phoning will feel bitterly hurt and disappointed they're not being written to or phoned.

And the one who just wants to get back to normal will feel irritated and finally downright annoyed because they feel they're being pestered!

So how *should* you handle a romance if you get yourself into one?

For a start try to admit, right from the first moment, that it *will* have a finishing time when the holiday's over.

Don't take it too seriously, particularly if you've got a

boyfriend of your own back home. In *that* particular situation you'll just feel guilt-ridden, and when the holiday's over and you've got to face your regular boy again, you'll probably make an utter fool of yourself by either being too stand-offish to begin with, or too over-enthusiastic! Then *he'll* guess something's happened — and the whole thing will be blown up into mammoth proportions!

If you daydream up a future, where the person you've met on a beach looking all tanned and healthy becomes more important than what he is — a person on a beach — you're in trouble. At home, when his tan fades, in *his* own setting — or even in yours — he could be an utterly deadly bore, and a couple of weeks where neither of you have to work or study isn't long enough in which to find that out!

In *real* life, he might have friends you detest, habits that drive you up the wall, or tastes you couldn't understand. And *you* might be just as dull and boring as far as he's concerned! But because you were both on holiday when you met, because you were both all out to enjoy yourselves, neither of you would notice the ordinary, everyday things.

A holiday romance that stays as just that, that's full of fun and sparkle but nothing more serious can be a great experience.

It can set you up for the

rest of the year, give you something to smile about all through the winter, *and* give you something to remember with real affection! In time, you may forget his name and even what he looks like if you don't have a photograph, but the sense of enjoyment should stick.

OK, so maybe you did fall in love with him just a little bit. Everybody does that now and then with all sorts of different people. But provided you're sensible enough to admit that someone you've met all too briefly *isn't* likely to turn into someone permanent in your life — you'll be home and dry.

And when the holiday itself is coming to an end, *don't* get too tearful and upset.

Swop addresses, by all means — but don't promise to write to him every single day.

Say you hope you'll see him again, by all means — but don't be too surprised if you never do.

Try to take the best out of your time together, but don't go crystal-gazing into the future and wondering if he has a part in it. The chances are he won't have and there's no point in ruining something perfectly good by over-reacting and trying to turn his friendship into something more than it probably is.

Stay cool, stay casual, and enjoy his company. Have a lot of laughs and do a lot of things together. But don't get too intense.

If you can manage all that, you'll go home having probably had the best holiday ever!

And there's always next year . . .

ONLY LOVE

"Daaahling," he breathes and 20 million women sigh. There's nothing like a good tear-jerker. Test your knowledge of the quivering lips and long, lingering looks in our sizzling screen romance quiz.

1. Jeremy Irons fell madly in love with 'The French Lieutenant's Woman'. Who was she played by?

2. Clark Gable didn't " give a damn " about whom in 'Gone With The Wind'?

3. A scantily clad Brooke Shields romped around in 'Blue Lagoon' with Christopher Atkins. Did he later become:
(a) Steven Carrington's boyfriend in 'Dynasty'?
(b) Sue Ellen's toy-boy in 'Dallas'?
(c) A long lost American cousin in the earlier episodes of 'Brookside'?

4. What was 'Brookside's' Heather Haversham's two-timing husband called and who was the business tycoon that she nearly married?

5. Terrorists burst in at the 'royal wedding' on 'Dynasty' and shot dead two people. Who?

6. Why was Corrie's Ken Barlow so upset when his daughter Susan started going out with Mike Baldwin?

7. Nana Mouskouri had a chart hit with 'Only Love' last year. Which TV mini-series was it the theme song of?

8. Billy Joel's girlfriend was played by his real-life wife Christie Brinkley in which of his videos?

ANSWERS

1. Meryl Streep.

2. Vivien Leigh.

3. (b) He was Pee-der, remember?

4. Hubbie was Roger Huntington, the guy she had a near-miss with was Tom Curzon.

5. Lady Ashley, and Steven's chum Luke.

6. (a) Because he was so much older than her and (b) because he's already had an affair with Deirdre, Ken's wife, and Ken thought Mike was only going out with Susan to get back at him.

7. 'Mistral's Daughter'

8. 'Uptown Girl'

9. (b) Australia.

10. Sandy (Remember, Sand-eee can't you seeee I'm in miseree . . .?)

11. Ali MacGraw.

12. (c) Romeo and Juliet.

13. 'Up Where We Belong,' by Joe Cocker.

14. 'As Time Goes By.'

15. 'From Here To Eternity.'

9. The kiss that shocked a nation of church-goers. Father Ralph smooched in the surf with Meggie in 'The Thorn Birds'. But in which country was it set?
(a) USA
(b) Australia
(c) South Africa.

10. 'Wella, wella, wella, oooh, tell me more, tell me more'. For a start, what was the name of Olivia Newton-John's character in 'Grease'?

11. 'Love Story', the seventies weepie, starred Ryan O'Neal and Ali MacGraw. At the end of the film one of them dies–which one?

12. 'West Side Story' was a modern-day musical based on:
(a) Antony and Cleopatra.
(b) Joan of Arc.
(c) Romeo and Juliet.

13. What was the theme song of Richard Gere's weepie 'An Officer And A Gentleman'?

14. In 'Casablanca' — the ultimate romantic film — what did Sam have to 'play again'?

15. Remember the kissing in the surf scene on the Bowie vid for 'China Girl' that was banned by the Beeb? From which film (starring Burt Lancaster) did this famous clinch originate?

SATURDAY NIG

Be a complete slob, and sit in front of the TV all night stuffing yourself.

Grab a sketch pad and draw all the members of the family.

Knit your dog or cat a tail-warmer for next winter.

Write down all Jonathan King's bad points — should take you all night.

Increase your stamina level by skipping for six minutes and stopping for 30 seconds after each minute, or by running up and down stairs for three minutes.

Treat the dog to a bath.

Write to Jackie.

Spend the night in the bath (don't tell the Beauty Ed. we told you so). Put Radox or bubble bath in the water and lie back with the radio or a tape playing in the background and a good book to read. So long as you keep topping up the water to keep it hot, you could stay there for hours.

Start knitting that jumper you've been eyeing up in the wool shop window for weeks.

Toons NOT to listen to . . .
1. *Alone Again (Naturally) — Gilbert O'Sullivan*
2. *Alone Without You — King*
3. *All By Myself — Eric Carmen*
4. *Me Myself I — Joan Armatrading*
5. *Are You Lonesome Tonight? — Elvis*
6. *Nobody's Child — Karen Young*
7. *Sing The Blues — Dave Edmunds*

Give yourself a full manicure and pedicure. (That's a manicure for your feet, in case you don't know).

Go through all your old photos and start a photo album.

Have a particularly wild party and wreck the house when your parents go out — this will occupy most of the Saturday nights for the next month as well, when they won't let you out.

Talk to the dog, the goldfish or the pot plant . . .

Go to bed at 6 p.m. and don't get up until 8 a.m. on Sunday morning!

Read your Jackie Annual.

Get yourself into the right state of mind and you can forget it's Saturday night at all. Instead, imagine it's Tuesday night — after all, who goes out on Tuesday nights apart from Jackie the Pop Ed? To authenticate your Saturday/Tuesday night, go to bed early after laying out your school uniform for the next day. Do this and you'll forget feeling depressed about staying in.

Make a list of all the things you'd like for next Christmas!

Draw a large mural on the living-room wall, incorporating artists' impressions of Paul King in the bath, etc. (Better ask your parents first!)

Sit and try to figure out the rules of American Football from the offical NFL league yearbook.

Answer all those letters you've been meaning to for ages. Catch up on the gossip with pen pals, old school mates or friends who have moved away — and why not suggest going out with them NEXT Saturday night! OK, so it may mean a bit of travelling but it'll be fun!

Stay in bed all day and refuse to acknowledge that it is Saturday.

Lie very quietly in a darkened room. If you ignore Saturday nights for long enough they might go away.

Have a good look in your mum and dad's wardrobe (better ask them first!) for any of their old clothes which you could adapt

Got nothing special to do on Saturday night? Lucky you, 'cos we've got some extra-special ideas . . .

into a pwetty twendy new outfit. Watch out for big baggy shirts, Dad's overcoats and suits, Mum's sixties minis or fifties frocks — even old brooches or scarves that could liven up something you already have.

...oons To Cheer You Up . . .
. My Favourite Things — Julie Andrews
2. Celebration — Kool and the Gang
3. Let's Go Crazy — Prince
4. Walking On Sunshine — Katrina and the Waves
.. Love Hangover — The Associates
.. Happy Talk — Captain Sensible
. We're All Going On A Summer Holiday — Cliff Richard

Read your old diaries or, if you haven't bothered to write one, why not have a look at the covers of your old school jotters to see who loved who then!

Make a list of all the boys you've ever gone out with, giving them marks out of ten for kissing, where they took you on dates, etc. Then write down their most disgusting habit and why you're better off without them! After all this lot, you'll be GLAD you're having a Saturday night in ALONE!

Tidy EVERYTHING! Your dressing table drawers, your records, your make-up, your clothes, your jewellery, in fact anything that needs tidying. At least you'll have achieved something!

Take over the kitchen and make your mum and dad supper. You don't have to be Delia Smith — cheese on toast will do, but it'll be appreciated.

Try to keep yourself occupied. You know the sort of thing — wander aimlessly around the house, count the flowers on the wall-paper, clean the budgie out (again), watch TV, put off doing your homework (again) . . .

Invite Aunt Beryl round for the evening. If you're going to be bored, you might as well do it properly.

Clear out all your old clothes, put them in a big black bag and give them away to Oxfam or something. It'll give you a clear wardrobe, an excuse for buying some new clothes and make you feel as though you've done something worthwhile.

Make your own scratch cassette — get a pile of records and a C60 cassette. The trick is to use the 'pause' button and just tape tiny little bits of a record onto the cassette. For instance the 'wooh whooh' bit in Bad Boys, or the 'sometimes you're better off dead . . .' bit from West End Girls. It'll take a bit of practise before you get it right, but when you do, you could be the next Malcolm McLaren or Paul Hardcastle.

Make a list of the places you could be going out to, but can't afford. It'll make you feel sick as a pig, but at least it'll pass the time.

Compile a list of the 'el doggiest' females in the whole world. Go on, get it out of your system and bitch away. Just who are the top ten biggest dogs in the world?

Go through all your old Jackies cutting out your favourite bits and making up a 'best of Jackie' scrapbook.

Write yourself a short story about a night out with Andrew Ridgeley. A real steamy Jackie Collins type thing — and who knows, we might even print it.

Get out the notepaper and write to anyone and everyone you can think of. Scour magazines for competitions and free offers — you never know, you might win something exciting.

Sit yourself in front of a mirror armed with all the make-up you can find and experiment with different looks, mixing different colours till you find a new you.

Reach for the old leotard and leg warmers, put on a good disco record and do half an hour of aerobics. After that, you'll feel all bright-eyed and bushy tailed (or at least you're supposed to). Remember to warm up and stretch the

muscles before you do anything too strenuous. Start off quite slowly and build up gradually to a faster pace then slow down gently. Never just 'stop' suddenly.

Start writing your memoirs so you can make a million when you become famous.

Phone up all your friends and see if any of them are sitting at home doing nothing as well. If so, go around to their house and have a good old bitching session.

Ten Boys You Wouldn't Mind Spending A Saturday Night In With . . .
1. **Andrew Ridgeley**
2. **Morten Harket (a-ha)**
3. **Mags Furuholmen (a-ha)**
4. **Pal Waaktaar (a-ha)**
5. **Michael J. Fox**
6. **John Taylor**
7. **Paul King**
8. **Simon Le Bon**
9. **Ian McCulloch (Echo and the Bunnyboys)**
10. **Ali Campbell (UB40)**

Offer to babysit your little sister so your mum and dad can go out and enjoy themselves . . . and give you some extra pocket money for being such a nice daughter so you can afford to go somewhere exciting next Saturday to make up for the boring time you're having this week.

Go out on your own. You don't need men to have a good time!

LAST CHRISTMAS

I'M SORRY WE WON'T SEE EACH OTHER AT CHRISTMAS, MOIRA, BUT YOU KNOW WHAT IT'S LIKE. MY FOLKS EXPECT ME TO SPEND IT WITH THEM DOWN IN CORNWALL. I'LL BE COMING BACK UP IN TIME FOR NEW YEAR, THOUGH.

THAT'S OK, COLIN. CHRISTMAS IS REALLY A FAMILY TIME ANYWAY, ISN'T IT?

I SUPPOSE SO. I'LL MISS YOU, THOUGH.

I'LL MISS YOU, TOO, BUT I'LL SEE YOU AT MY NEW YEAR'S EVE PARTY. OH . . . AND JUST IN CASE WE CAN'T GET THROUGH TO EACH OTHER ON THE BIG DAY . . . HAPPY CHRISTMAS!

HAPPY CHRISTMAS, MOIRA.

IT'LL BE A LOT HAPPIER THAN LAST CHRISTMAS, ANYWAY. I STILL HAVE BAD DREAMS ABOUT IT. BUT IT'S OVER NOW . . . I DON'T WANT TO START THINKING ABOUT ALL THAT AGAIN . . .

THERE WAS STILL A LOT TO DO BEFORE THE BIG DAY . . .

WE'VE USUALLY GOT THE DECORATIONS UP BY NOW.

I'LL DO IT, MUM. I LOVE HANGING DECORATIONS. AND SUZY'S COMING OVER THIS AFTERNOON, SO SHE CAN HELP ME.

SO . . .

COLIN ISN'T GOING TO BE HERE FOR CHRISTMAS, THEN?

NO, HE'S SPENDING IT WITH HIS FOLKS. I SUPPOSE MOST UNIVERSITY STUDENTS GO HOME AT CHRISTMAS, DON'T THEY?

YOU'VE BEEN GOING OUT WITH COLIN FOR A WHILE NOW. IT MUST BE STARTING TO GET SERIOUS, EH?

I HOPE SO. IT'S MEANT A LOT TO ME THIS YEAR, MEETING SOMEONE LIKE HIM. I DON'T KNOW IF I'D HAVE GOT OVER IT WITHOUT HIM.

YOU MEAN WHAT HAPPENED LAST CHRISTMAS — WHEN THERE WAS ALL THE TROUBLE BETWEEN YOU AND DEREK?

WELL . . . SORT OF. WE HAD OUR FIRST QUARREL ON CHRISTMAS DAY, ANYWAY. BUT IT WAS NEW YEAR'S EVE BEFORE WE FINALLY SPLIT UP.

BUT IT'S TIME I FORGOT ALL THAT. I'M HAPPY NOW, WITH COLIN . . . AND THIS CHRISTMAS IS THE TIME WHEN I FINALLY BURY THE PAST FOR GOOD . . .

THEN . . .

OH, GOOD. THE POSTIE'S DELIVERED SOME MORE CARDS.

IT — IT CAN'T BE . . . IT CAN'T . . .!

WHAT IS IT, MOIRA? WHO'S IT FROM?

IT'S DEREK'S WRITING! I'D KNOW IT ANYWHERE!

With Best Wishes for Christmas And the New Year

MERRY CHRISTMAS FROM DEREK

X X X

BUT THAT — THAT'S IMPOSSIBLE . . . IT CAN'T BE . . .!

MRS BLACK! COME QUICK!

MOIRA'S PARENTS CAME RUNNING . . .

IT'S SOME SORT OF SICK PRACTICAL JOKE. IT'S JUST SOMEONE DISGUISING THEIR WRITING TO LOOK LIKE DEREK'S.

NO. IT'S DEREK'S WRITING ON THAT CARD. I KNOW IT IS!

BUT IT CAN'T BE, MOIRA. DEREK'S DEAD! HE DIED NEARLY A YEAR AGO!

BUT IT'S HIS WRITING! IT'S DEREK'S WRITING!

MOIRA, DEREK'S DEAD. YOU KNOW HE IS. YOU WERE AT THE FUNERAL.

SHE'S REALLY UPSET, MRS BLACK. IT — IT'S AWFUL THAT SOMETHING LIKE THIS SHOULD HAVE TO HAPPEN NOW, JUST WHEN SHE WAS STARTING TO GET OVER IT ALL . . .

I KNOW, SUZY. SHE WAS SO LOOKING FORWARD TO CHRISTMAS, TOO . . .

CONTINUED ON PAGE 58

LATER . . .

IT'S DEREK'S WRITING, I KNOW IT IS! BUT HOW CAN IT BE? I WISH COLIN WAS HERE. MAYBE I'LL PHONE HIM TOMORROW. I WON'T TELL HIM WHAT'S HAPPENED, THOUGH. HE'LL ONLY WORRY, AND THERE'S NO POINT SPOILING HIS CHRISTMAS, TOO.

SO . . .

WHAT ARE YOUR PLANS FOR TONIGHT, THEN?

I'M GOING OUT WITH SUZY AND A COUPLE OF GIRLS. I — I MISS YOU. NEW YEAR'S EVE CAN'T COME QUICKLY ENOUGH, SO I CAN SEE YOU AGAIN.

THAT EVENING . . .

YOU'RE NOT STILL THINKING ABOUT THAT CARD YOU GOT, ARE YOU?

I CAN'T HELP IT. IT ALMOST MADE ME FEEL LIKE HE'D COME BACK TO HAUNT ME . . .

OH, DON'T BE SILLY. IT WAS JUST SOMEONE'S IDEA OF A JOKE, THAT'S ALL.

BUT DON'T YOU REMEMBER WHAT HAPPENED LAST YEAR? AFTER THAT ARGUMENT, I DIDN'T SEE DEREK AGAIN UNTIL HE TURNED UP AT THE NEW YEAR'S EVE PARTY. HE STARTED RAVING AND SHOUTING, AND I TOLD HIM WE WERE FINISHED FOR GOOD. AND — AND THAT WAS THE LAST TIME I SAW HIM. ON THE WAY HOME HE . . . HE CRASHED THE CAR . . .

I ALMOST BLAMED MYSELF FOR HIS DEATH. I THOUGHT IT MIGHT NOT HAVE HAPPENED IF I HADN'T SPLIT WITH HIM. MAYBE THAT'S WHY IT TOOK ME SO LONG TO GET OVER IT.

WELL, AT LEAST NOTHING ELSE HAS HAPPENED SINCE YOU GOT THAT CARD. JUST TRY TO FORGET IT AND ENJOY YOURSELF.

ON CHRISTMAS MORNING . . .

THIS ONE'S FROM ME, LOVE, AND THAT'S FROM YOUR MOTHER.

THANKS, DAD. HERE'S YOURS. I JUST HOPE IT'S THE RIGHT SIZE!

OH, THIS ONE'S GOT MY NAME ON IT TOO. WHO'S IT FROM?

IT'LL BE FROM UNCLE PETER, I EXPECT.

IT — IT CAN'T BE! IT LOOKS EXACTLY LIKE THE RING DEREK ALWAYS USED TO WEAR . . . AND THE CARD'S IN HIS HANDWRITING AGAIN! IT . . . IT SAYS HE'LL SEE ME AT NEW YEAR!

Life is what you make it, so make your New Year's resolution to be positive . . . and make the most of your life!

go for it!

The need for approval

You go into town on Saturday afternoon and buy yourself a bright yellow baggy T-shirt. It looks great with your white leggings and you feel like a million dollars. That evening at the disco your friend (?) says, "You look like a pregnant canary!" Do you:

(a) Leave in tears, and use the T-shirt as a floorcloth?

(b) Stay, feeling awful, and decide to take it to the Oxfam shop on Monday?

(c) Resolve only to wear it when you're not out with that particular friend?

(d) Say, "Well, that's your opinion, but I took ages choosing it and I think it looks great."?

If you need the approval of other people you're saying, in effect, "I can't trust my own judgement. Other people's opinions are more important than my own."

Wrong. Don't give in to feelings of self-doubt. **You** are the most important person in your life. Take control of it, and don't let someone else's remarks — whether well-meant or catty — make you doubt yourself.

Remember, you can never please everyone, so why try? In fact, if you please half of the people you're doing well, so just remind yourself you've run into one of those people in the 50 per cent who don't agree with you.

Ask yourself one important question. If your friend had approved of your T-shirt, would you have been better off? The answer, of course, is no. Whatever she thinks, it can have no effect on you — unless you let it!

Fear of the unknown

Your boyfriend works out at the gym three times a week. The closest you ever come to exercise is the four-minute dash to the bathroom in the morning. He asks you to go to the mixed session at the gym with him. Do you:

(a) Pack him in and start dating a slob?

(b) Rush to the chemist's and buy a crepe bandage, saying you've sprained your ankle?

(c) Promise you'll go with him — **after** you've lost half a stone?

(d) Dig out your leotard and legwarmers, and just go?

Unless you open yourself up to new experiences, you'll lead a pretty dull life, and you'll become a bore. There are too many people who live their life rigidly, never exploring anything new, never

doing anything spontaneously, always playing safe. Take a good look at them. Do you want to become like them, spiritless, never taking a chance? Of course you don't.

Let's say you go to the gym and you hate it. So what? It's maybe two hours out of your life — that's not the end of the world. What would you have been doing otherwise? Watching EastEnders? Cutting your toenails?

Who knows, there's always a chance that once you've entered into the world of clanking weights and gleaming chrome machines, you might just find it's the kind of sport you've been looking for. It can help you get — and stay — fit, reshape your figure, and it's a great way of spending time with your boyfriend. What have you got to lose?

Maybe you're frightened to go because you think you won't be any good at it. Don't equate your success in the gym with your own self-worth. Not to succeed in a particular activity is not to fail as a person. It just means you're not successful with that particular activity at that particular moment. Pop groups make records; if they don't make Number One the first time, they release another, and another. They don't sit there and whine, complaining about the hit that never was.

So bring a little colour into your life. Take a few risks. Remember, it's **your** life, and it's the Real Thing — not a dress rehearsal!

Worry and jealousy — useless emotions

You've been dead keen on a boy for ages. Now he's asked you to a party on Saturday. Great! Except that your friend also fancies him and you know she'll do

everything to lure him away from you. Do you:

(a) Stay at home and blubber, and let them get on with it?

(b) Tell him you get claustrophobic at parties and suggest a night at the pictures?

(c) Slap on the warpaint, go out and flirt with every boy in sight?

(d) Stay cool and decide to have a wonderful time — whatever happens?

You're worrying yourself witless about the party. Why? Will it make things any better? Of course not. It may give you frown lines, but if you spent your whole life worrying about the future, it still wouldn't change a thing.

When you catch yourself worrying about a problem, ask yourself this question:

Is there anything I can do to alter the situation?

If the answer is no, then stop worrying — it's useless.

If the answer is yes, then do it, change things to suit you better.

Let's imagine you arrive at the party and your friend makes a bee-line for your boy. One of two things could happen:

(1) He's pleasant to her, but makes it clear he's with you.

(2) He forgets about you and disappears into the distance with her.

If you're a positive person, you should react the same way in either situation. You are your own person. You don't belong to anyone else, and no one else belongs to you. You are a self-contained unit. If he chooses to go with your friend, that's **his** decision. It has nothing to do with you. You enjoyed life before you met him, you can enjoy life now. Your feeling of security should come **from within yourself,** not be dependent on someone else's behaviour.

By comparing yourself to your friend and imagining you are liked less, you're saying she is more important than you. You are measuring your own worth in comparison to your friend. Tell yourself that someone can always choose another person without it being a reflection on you.

If you learn to like yourself, you'll believe so much in **you** that you won't need the love or approval of others to give you value. So jealousy, which comes from a lack of self-confidence, can be banished from your life altogether.

It's all part of being in control of your life, of your feelings, your destiny. Once you learn to be more assertive (and that **doesn't** mean being aggressive!), you'll find you like yourself more. And it follows that other people will like you more, too!

City slickers and country cousins.
We take a closer look at the lifestyles
of two Jackie readers . . .

COUNTRY G

NAME: Donna Campbell

Age: 17

HOMETOWN: St Cyrus (A tiny village in the north of Scotland).

OCCUPATION: I'm still at school, but I have a sort of part-time job helping my dad on the farm.

HOBBIES: I like watching TV — especially all the soaps, apart from Emmerdale Farm, which I hate. It's nothing at all like real life on a farm. Apart from that, I spend quite a lot of my time with my horse Norman!

FAVOURITE POP BANDS: I like a lot of things in the charts — especially Phil Collins and Dire Straits. A lot of people think they're boring and old-fashioned but at least they can play their instruments.

HOW MUCH MONEY DO YOU HAVE TO SPEND PER WEEK? Not very much! If I help my dad around the farm he gives me a tenner. I don't have to pay board or anything — well, not until I get a proper job.

WHAT DO YOU SPEND IT ON? Mostly clothes as there aren't that many other things to spend money on around here. I spend a lot of money on books and magazines as well. I think Mills and Boon have made a fortune out of me! I don't have to buy clothes for during the day as we've to wear uniform, and my mum pays for that.

WHAT'S YOUR FAVOURITE SHOP FOR CLOTHES? Because I don't get into town that often I get a lot of my things from catalogues. People slag them off but they do have some nice stuff — Freemans especially. When I'm in town I quite like places like Top Shop.

DESCRIBE A TYPICAL DAY IN YOUR LIFE: We all get up pretty early — that's my mum and dad, my two older brothers and me. My mum forces me to eat a cooked breakfast before I go to school, as she believes you can't get through the day without it. I get the bus to school which can sometimes take over half an hour.

In the morning, it's mostly the academic things like Maths and English while the afternoon is lighter subjects. Despite what you might think we don't have a village school with 3 or 4 pupils. I go to the local Academy which has a few hundred pupils.

When I come home from school I help out on the farm, tidying up, etc., and try to spend some time with my horse. After teatime I've got quite a lot of homework for my Highers, although I tend to watch too much TV instead of concentrating on my homework — I can't miss EastEnders!

I don't really go out during the week as there's not that much to do Monday to Friday — and besides I couldn't afford it.

WHAT DO YOU DO ON A SATURDAY NIGHT? I'm quite lucky as my boyfriend's got a car so he drives me into the disco in the town. I really like getting dressed up on a Saturday night out so it takes me about three hours to get ready. He picks me up about eight and then we head into town to meet his pal and his girlfriend. I get home about 1 or 2 o'clock, which my mum and dad don't mind too much.

DO YOU HAVE A BOYFRIEND? As I mentioned before, yes. His name's Neil, he's 21 and works as a mechanic in the next village. We see each other about two or three times week and have been going out now for over a year.

CAN YOU SEE YOURSELF GETTING MARRIED? Not to Neil, don't think, but I will get married — probably when I'm about 20 — if I get the offer!

WHAT'S THE BEST THING ABOU LIVING IN THE COUNTRY? You get to know everyone here — there' hardly any strangers. Everyone's friendly so there's hardly any trouble with vandalism and drugs, etc.

DO YOU THINK YOU'D BE ABLE TO SURVIVE LIVING IN THE TOWN? I'd like to have a bash sometime, but I don't know if I'd like to live there.

AME: Hayley Grant

GE: 17

OMETOWN: Birmingham.

CCUPATION: Clerical assistant in insurance company.

OBBIES: Listening to music, going discos, watching videos, keep fit — I go to a class with the girls from e office — and going on holiday. I to Spain every year!

AVOURITE POP BANDS: I like ost disco music, things like Five ar, Madonna, Whitney Houston and eorge Benson. But I also enjoy ancing to groups like Simple Minds d Talking Heads.

OW MUCH MONEY DO YOU AVE TO SPEND PER WEEK? fter I've given my mum her board oney and put away enough to buy y bus pass, I usually have around 5 a week to spend. I get paid onthly, though, so it doesn't always ork out like that — it depends on hat I have to buy that month.

HAT DO YOU SPEND IT ON? oing out mostly. I usually go out all ree nights at the weekend and once uring the week, so that costs quite a

lot. I also buy a lot of clothes both for discos and for work — we have to dress smartly in the office so I'm forever buying new blouses and skirts! I try and save some, too, for holidays and things.

WHAT'S YOUR FAVOURITE SHOP FOR CLOTHES? I like most of the chain stores — Top Shop, Chelsea Girl and Clockhouse at C&A are good. If I want something really special, for a wedding or something, I'll go to Next.

DESCRIBE A TYPICAL DAY IN YOUR LIFE: I usually get up around quarter past eight — which is quite late seeing as I get the bus at twenty five to nine! I don't have time for breakfast, but I grab a filled roll at coffee break at ten o'clock. I'm kept really busy at work, typing letters, filing and making cups of tea for the clients. We get an hour for lunch, so I either look around the shops or go for a bar lunch with a few of the girls from my office. Our afternoons are our busiest time — that's when we get all the phone calls and process all the claims — so by the time we finish at five o'clock, I'm really quite tired. I go home, have my tea, and then I usually phone a few of my mates to see what's happening — we sometimes go to the pictures or

round to each other's houses for a gossip. I never go to bed late, if it's any later than half past ten, I'd never be able to get up in the morning!

WHAT DO YOU DO ON A SATURDAY NIGHT? I hit the town with my mates! Mostly, we go to a disco — they're all over-eighteen nightclubs, but I don't drink so my mum doesn't mind me going. As long as she knows I'll get a taxi home with a friend, she's quite happy. If it's a friend's birthday or a special occasion, we go for a Chinese meal and we've been invited to quite a few eighteenth birthday parties recently — all my pals are getting old!

DO YOU HAVE A BOYFRIEND? No, and I'm quite happy about it! I have a great time going out with my mates and I know I wouldn't be able to do that as much if I had a steady boyfriend. We all fancy certain boys, and there's a couple of guys who walk me home if I meet them at discos, but I don't want to get involved with anyone at the moment.

CAN YOU SEE YOURSELF GETTING MARRIED? Not for years and years and years! I suppose eventually I'll settle down, but I've no plans for anything like that yet.

WHAT ARE YOUR PLANS FOR THE FUTURE? I'd like a better job — maybe something in an advertising agency, and I wouldn't mind going down to London if I had to. It would be fantastic to earn enough to go on two holidays a year!

WHAT'S THE BEST THING ABOUT LIVING IN THE CITY? Having loads to do! I get bored really easily so I love doing lots of different things. The city's definitely a great place when you're young.

DO YOU THINK YOU'D BE ABLE TO SURVIVE LIVING IN THE COUNTRY? No way! I can't imagine anything worse! What would you do at the weekends? Somehow I can't imagine me at a barn dance or fancying a young farmer! I went on a driving holiday with my parents when I was younger and we toured all round the countryside, honestly, it was the worst time of my life — all those cows and trees and grass, it gave me hayfever!

HAT TRICKS

FIONA WILDE, from Catford, is a dancer. The fake fur hat was a bargain from a Miss Selfridge sale about four years ago . . . when not in fur, she likes to tilt a huge, blue trilby over one eye for a mysterious look.

Q. What do you need to see you through Winter in style?

a) A crateful of Wispa bars and a hot water bottle?
b) A thermal vest and ribby longjohns?
c) A hat?

A. All of these, actually, but we decided to find out more about hats . . .

DEE & SCARLETT are both 18 and both from Bournemouth. "Hats are an integral part of an outfit," Dee explains. "I make hats to go with everything! My most outrageous is a theatrical gold brocade one . . ."

JERRY, from Oxford, has just swiped this skipper's cap from a friend. "It's a nice hat — I hope she'll let me keep it. It keeps my hair up."

ANGELA MACDONALD, 21, from Broughty Ferry, went to Art College in Dundee and now works as a junior designer for Conran Associates in London. "I like chips, free drinks, Duran Duran and designing party posters. I hate people who take themselves too seriously, and Sushi — that's Japanese for raw fish. My hat and gloves are by Naf Naf — I bought them 'cos I wanted to be cheered up!"

ELAYNA, 16, from Kilburn, was taking a sneaky break from college to watch the buskers in Covent Garden. "Can't remember where I got the hat — I don't usually wear one but I've run out of hairspray today. My plait's real, by the way — none of your fake plastic jobs, this. It took a lifetime to grow."

YUKA SARASHINA, from Japan, is staying with friends in Brixton. The hat's from Japan — Yuki cut the holes in it herself and customised with badges and artistic wisps of hair. "I love Brixton, hats, David Bowie, and . . . having my photo taken!"

We tell you how to get a good night's sleep . . .

Do you toss and turn for hours before falling asleep at nights? If so, our hints on getting to sleep could be just what you need!

Sensible ways to get to sleep.

First of all, make sure your bed's comfortable. If it's too soft, you don't have to get a new bed, but you may need a new mattress.

Here's an old-fashioned one. Soak a long cotton sock in cold water, and wring it out completely. Put it on your foot, and cover it with a dry sock. Then crawl into bed. It's an old wives' tale, but it works because the cold stimulates the circulation, drawing blood down from the head, which makes you drowsy. Try it, it really does work!

Milk can have a soporific effect (that means it can help you get to sleep)! A cup of drinking chocolate (try Cadbury's Bournvita) last thing at night makes a soothing nightcap. Make it with all milk or half milk and half water. Slowly heat the milk or milk and water in a pan, but don't allow it to boil. Put 1½-2½ teaspoons of drinking chocolate or Bournvita in a mug and add a bit of sugar if you like. Add a pinch of ground cinnamon and lots of ground nutmeg (you can grate your own nutmeg with a cheese grater if you want it to be really fresh). Pour the milk into a mug, and sprinkle some chocolate chips on top, if you want to be a real pig! It helps if you eat something, like a couple of digestive biscuits with your nightcap to absorb the milk, but remember — they won't do anything for your figure!

Other drinks which have a soporific effect are teas made from lime, lemon balm, camomile and passion flower. You can buy these from most health-food shops. It's possible to buy passion-flower, or "Passiflora" tablets in some chemists, which are natural and non-addictive sleep-inducing tablets. You can also buy pleasant tasting mixtures of these teas from health food shops, specially prepared for inducing sleep. Look out for "Sleepytime" and "Goodnight".

Read a book. Don't choose one that you just can't put down, though, or you'll stay up till the early hours trying to finish it, and if you do turn in, you'll be unable to sleep out of suspense! Read something uncomplicated, like Jackie Collins — that'll soon send you to sleep!

get into your lazy bed

Avoid drinking tea or coffee after 6.00 in the evening. They contain a lot of caffeine, which is a stimulant, and just one cup of strong coffee or tea (this doesn't include herb or fruit teas, of course) can keep you awake for up to six hours! Try avoiding tea or coffee altogether (or have a cup first thing in the morning, to get you going), and see how much more relaxed you feel.

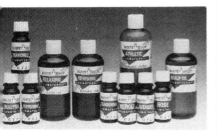

(Love the pic! — The Ed.)

Try some oils from the "Aromatherapy" range at the Body Shop. Lavender, Camomile, or Neroli are good, or try their relaxing Bath Oil in a hot bath before you go to bed.

Hops, a plant of the mulberry family used for flavouring beer and medicine, can help induce sleep. These are available from most health food shops, and you'll need LOTS of them! Boil a small panful of them in about two cups of water to make a truly foul-tasting drink which you can sweeten with sugar or honey. But it'll put you out like a light!

With your eyes shut tightly, try to look at the insides of your eyelids. On the imaginary "screen", imagine you're drawing a picture with a line of green fluorescent. It really works, honest!

Repeat the word "soporific" slowly and methodically to yourself for three minutes before you drop off. This will clear your mind of all disturbing thoughts and help you to relax. In case you get too used to the word and start to think of other things while you're repeating it, change your word every few days. Choose sleepy words, like snooze, doze, somnolence, laziness, drowsiness, heaviness, sluggish, indolence, langour, lethargy, dreaminess, sleepiness, fatigue, yawning, slumber, somnambulism, sedative, anaesthetic, dreamland, relaxation, lullaby, lazybones, sleepwalking, loungeabout, sleepyhead, dormouse, drifting, floating, comatose, somniferous, hypnotic, loitering, or dozing.

Think about your breathing pattern: how long it takes you in second counts to inhale and exhale, inhale, exhale, inhale . . . zzzzzzz!

Get into a nice, warm bed, and snuggle up. Then, close your eyes and imagine the alarm clock's just rung and you've got to get up and go to school/work. You're late, the car's broken down and the buses aren't running, and there's no hot water, and no time for breakfast. You just want to turn over, and go back to sleep . . .

Silly ways to get to sleep.

Intead of counting sheep, count how many boys you know that you might go out with if they asked *really* nicely . . .

Hit your head against the bedroom wall thirty times; you're bound to knock yourself out sometime.

Put on a Barry White single at 33⅓ rpm. Guaranteed to send you into a sound slumber before it's finished playing!

WINTER . . . and snow. Tall, ghostly trees, their branches brushed with white. The park like a giant iced birthday cake, its candles all blown out. A flurry of thin white clouds across the moon. Then snowflakes falling, falling everywhere . . .

That was the night when I walked home with Paul. That was the night the world turned upside-down. When everything held a new, exciting meaning . . . when I knew that nothing would be the same again.

I'd gone to Jane's party half-reluctantly. Wondering if my white dress suited me . . . wishing I had a new and trendy hair-style. Knowing I'd be the youngest person there — because Jane was my older sister's friend, not mine. Still, if it was really awful I could slip out early, catch the last bus home. I could sit in the dark and watch the midnight movie . . . or close my eyes and dream my dreams of Paul . . .

Paul had been in my dreams for a long, long time. Destined to stay there, too — well, so I'd thought. How *could* he guess the way I felt about him when we'd only seen each other in a crowd? My sister's crowd and Jane's . . .

Yet somehow . . . somehow the miracle had happened. Here I was — and it was long past midnight — walking across the still, white park with him. Watching the snowflakes falling on his hair. Watching his profile — handsome, remote, like a profile on a coin. Waiting for him to speak, wondering if he knew how I felt about him. And how he felt about me . . .

I watched the snowflakes settling in his hair and smiled . . .

I could so easily have missed that party. I hadn't dared to ask my sister, Margot, if Paul would be there. I'd wanted to ask but I couldn't trust my voice. However casual I tried to make it, it cracked in the strangest way whenever it came out with Paul's name.

And Margot, who was the kind who noticed things, had teased me about it . . . had even gone so far as to warn me off . . . *"Now look, little sister, Paul's a nice enough guy, but he's no prince in shining armour. And, believe me, he's no baby-snatcher, either . . ."*

Not that it mattered a bit what Margot said. There were times when I'd found myself almost pitying Margot. Margot, at seventeen, changed her boyfriends more often than her hairstyles . . . She'd never known what it was to be in love. She couldn't even hope to understand what I, who was two years younger, felt about Paul.

I watched the snowflakes settling on his hair and smiled as I thought again about the party. Remembering every detail, every word . . .

I'd noticed him the moment I'd arrived. And because he was Paul — lean and blond and handsome — plenty of other girls had noticed him, too. Watching him drift around from group to group, discussing him among themselves, I thought. Their voices light and casual and uncaring, their eyes alert and hopeful.

A few of Margot's friends had pulled me up to dance with them, to be kind to the shy kid-sister. But my dancing had been half-hearted, automatic — and all the time I'd been looking out for Paul. Conscious of where he was, who he was with — yet pretending all the time that I hadn't noticed.

I told them after a while that I was tired — and this was quite true. There's something really tiring about pretending. They left me alone after that. I went to the cloakroom and fixed my hair to pass the time away. It was restful in there — away from the lights and the heavy throb of the music. I didn't have to keep smiling all the time, smiling and smiling like my face would crack . . . I didn't need to hide my disappointment.

By the time I joined the crowd again I wasn't disappointed anymore, just resigned. The party was almost over, after all. If anything wonderful had been going to happen it would have happened by now . . .

THEN I saw him. Paul. I glimpsed him out of the corner of my eye as I stood by the window, looking at the snow. And I saw that he was walking in my direction. Coming to me — just as, deep down, I'd always known he would.

"Hi, Clare," he said. "How come you're all alone?"

I'd turned round slowly then and smiled at him. And suddenly felt mysterious, beautiful — my dress a snow-white cloud . . . my hair a dark curtain, sleek like satin . . .

He'd smiled back. Somehow I'd felt that this smile of his was something that no-one else had ever seen. A different smile, especially for me.

"It's pretty late," he said. "I'll walk you home."

I'd collected my coat and bag as if in a dream, yet aware of the envious stares that followed me as I left the party with Paul.

Somehow we hadn't talked a lot at first. I wanted to make the most of every moment, but it was hard to think of things to say. But once in the park with the snowflakes whirling around us, enclosing us in our own little private world, talking was easy. And there was something which I had to tell him — something which seemed quite suddenly important.

"I had a snowstorm once — a plastic one. I won it at a party years ago — when I was a kid. There were these prizes, you see — I forget what for . . ."

I felt his eyes smiling at me through the snowflakes. Funny, I thought, how close you felt to someone when you were telling things about your childhood . . .

My mind went racing back across the years to the long, bright room, the candles on the cake, the red balloons, the sea of up-turned faces . . . *"You've won! You've won a prize, Clare . . . come and get it!"*

I saw myself again at five years old — shy, hesitant, uncertain. Remembered the crackle of the wrapping-paper, my sudden little tingle of excitement.

I'd been a bit disappointed just at first. Not so exciting, after all, I'd thought. Two tiny figures in a plastic bubble . . .

"You turn it upside down," someone had said.

Specially written for Jackie by Elizabeth Farrant.

And it was then the magic had begun. A miracle, a fairy tale come true. Two tiny figures in a whirl of snowflakes. No ordinary couple, I was certain. One was a princess in a long, white gown — that was myself, of course. The other was a prince — lean, blond and handsome, no-one I recognised. But I'd known that I'd find him — this year, next year, sometime . . .

And so I had.

He said — and now his lips were smiling, too — "And you turned it over every other minute. Because you had to keep the snowflakes falling?"

I nodded quickly — he understood so well. "How did you guess?"

"Because you're a dreamer, Clare —

you always were. And because you want every dream to last for ever. Just like a fairy tale . . ."

I wanted to cry as I watched him walk away.

Voices half-lost among a whirl of snowflakes.

I tried to keep my own relaxed and steady. "But . . . doesn't everyone?" I asked. "Don't *you*?"

He squeezed my hand. "Forever's a long, long time," he told me quietly.

We walked in silence till we reached my gate. I was content for it to be that way. I didn't want to talk. It was enough to feel I was here with Paul . . . that the magic of the night was all around us and the world was upside-down and the snowflakes falling . . .

But it stopped quite suddenly. There was scarcely a single snowflake falling now. The sky would be clear quite soon — the stars would shine.

"Only a shower," he said. "It's over now."

It was over and the magic had gone. Now I was no-one special, after all. No-one mysterious or beautiful. I was only Clare — the girl who dreamed too much, who wanted every dream to last for ever.

I looked at the empty sky and tried to smile. I said, "I'd have liked to keep the snowflakes falling."

"You're funny, Clare," he told me. "Funny — but sweet."

He kissed me very gently on the cheek. "Don't stay too long in that plastic bubble of yours. Remember there's a lot of world outside . . ."

And then he was gone.

I wanted to cry as I watched him walk away. But not because he was walking out of my life, as they say in stories. He wasn't, of course — he'd never walked into it, not really.

But because I'd never had the chance to tell him that this was the night the world turned upside-down . . .●

how do you feel about black cats?

Cross your fingers, touch wood, and find out your superstition rating!

Are you the sort of person who'd spend hours in a field searching for a four-leafed clover? Do you avoid walking under ladders at all costs, even if it means walking in the middle of a busy road? Or would you not even bat an eyelid if there was a ladder over your head? In other words, how superstitious are you? Read on, and find out . . .

1. While taking a walk in the country, you see an acorn lying on the ground. Do you:
(a) leave it exactly where it is, as picking up an acorn is extremely unlucky,
(b) feed it to the squirrels,
(c) pop it into your handbag, or
(d) put it behind your ear to prevent deafness in later life?

2. After a relative's wedding, you come home with a piece of wedding cake. Do you:
(a) eat it for tea,
(b) feed it to the boy you fancy like mad so that he'll be yours for eternity,
(c) keep it for seven years and seven days to ensure good luck, or
(d) put it under your pillow, so that you'll dream of the man you'll marry?

3. A black cat crosses your path. Do you feel:
(a) not really bothered. It just means the neighbours are feeding the strays again,
(b) pleased, as it's very lucky,
(c) a bit frightened — it means there's a witches' coven not far away, or,
(d) upset; it's very unlucky?

4. What would you say to your friend to wish her luck if she was just about to make her first entrance on stage in the school play?
(a) "Shake a leg!",
(b) "Break a leg!",
(c) "May the spirit of Macbeth ne'er haunt you!", or
(d) "Go on, do your best, I know you can!"?

5. All vegetables are good for you, but eating carrots improves:
(a) your greengrocer's profits,
(b) your eyesight,
(c) your love life, or
(d) all of these?

6. Mum buys you a lovely green dress. What's your reaction?
(a) "It's lovely, but I can't wear it! It's unlucky!",
(b) "That'll look great with my new green shoes!", or
(c) "Great! I'll wear it to the disco on Friday! As Granny says, 'Girls who wear green are every boy's dream!'"?

7. Mum brings some May Blossom into the house and puts it in a vase. What do you think about it?
(a) "She must have taken up flower arranging",
(b) "Get rid of it quick! It'll bring trouble!", or
(c) "What a lucky flower to have in the house!"?

8. When are you most likely to see a werewolf?
(a) Every time there's a new moon,
(b) Every time there's a full moon,
(c) During an old Boris Karloff horror film, or
(d) walking through a graveyard at midnight on the night of the Winter Solstice?

9. Why would a boy sleep with an orange under his armpit?
(a) Because he's some kind of nutter,
(b) To prevent B.O.,
(c) To help him gain the love of the girl he desires?

10. A friend is anxious to keep evil spirits and vampires away form her house, after staying up too often to watch the late night horror films. What would you advise her to hang over the doors and window for her protection?
(a) Potato peelings,
(b) Curtains,
(c) Garlic,
(d) A picture of Princess Diana, to counter evil with goodness and purity?

Scoring

1. a) 1, b) 0, c) 2, d) 1. Carrying an acorn around with you is supposed to prevent you from growing old.

2. a) 0, b) 1, c) 1, d) 2. d) is the correct answer.

3. a) 0, b) 2, c) 2, d) 1. A black cat crossing your path is a lucky sign, although in the old days it was often thought that witches took the form of cats sometimes, so the presence of a cat could mean that there was a witches' coven nearby.

4. a) 1, b) 2. c) 1, d) 0. b) is correct. This common custom among actors may derive from the fact that it's meant to be lucky if an actor falls, accidentally, on stage. Stumbling, however, is unlucky, and means that the actor is likely to fluff his lines. Answer c) was put in to confuse you. The Shakespeare play "Macbeth" is thought to be very unlucky, as the witches' song in the play is thought to have the power of working evil.

5. a) 0, b) 2, c) 2, d) 3. Superstition says that carrots can improve your eyesight AND your love life, and scientists agree that they are good for the eyes.

6. a) 2, b) 0, c) 1. Fooled you! a) is correct.

7. a) 0, b) 2, c) 1. Never bring May Blossom into the house.

8. a) 1, b) 2, c) 0, d) 1. b) is superstitiously correct.

9. a) 0, b) 1, c) 2. Ancient custom says that if a man wants to win a girl's heart, he should take an orange and prick it all over its skin with a needle. He must then sleep with it under his armpit. Next day he should give it to the girl without telling her why, and where it has been all night, and if she agrees to eat it, she will return his love.

10. a) 1, b) 0, c) 2, d) 1. Evil spirits don't like garlic.

Conclusions

15-21: You certainly know your superstitions. You're probably up early every May 1st, washing your face in the morning dew, and you probably wander round with your eyes shut on Valentine's Day until you know the boy you fancy is standing in front of you (the first bloke you see on Valentine's Day is your future husband). But don't take things too far. You must've heard the story about the man who stepped off a pavement to avoid walking under a ladder. He got run over by a bus . . .

8-14: Superstition doesn't dominate your life, thank goodness, because you've got a habit of getting your superstitions a bit muddled! You'd probably be overjoyed if you found a lucky horseshoe, but you wouldn't be thrown into the depths of depression just because it was Friday 13th.

0-7: You're not in the least bit superstitious, and probably go out of your way to prove it by defiantly walking under ladders when everyone else is going out of their way to avoid them, and spilling salt without throwing some over your shoulder. You probably like hockey and computers, and wearing tank tops. But we bet you take a wee peek at your horoscope now and then . . .

HOW TO ASK HIM OUT

... and persuade him to say yes!

OK, so you've come to the conclusion that he's A Bit of All Right. You've peered at him across the dance floor. You've spent a bus journey studying the back of his neck, missing your stop in the process. You've taken up 'him' as a hobby instead of breeding tropical fish. And although you may not be in love, you're definitely on the way.

We've all been in the situation at some time or another. And usually, if worshipping him secretly from afar is about as close to getting to know him as you've ever been, it'll take a miracle to bring the two of you together.

Perhaps, then, there's something to be said for plucking up your courage and making your interest more obvious.

Naturally, there's showing you're interested and showing you're interested! He'll hardly throw himself at your feet if you can't pluck up the courage to squeak "hello" when you run into each other in the library, but he'll more than likely turn on his heels and scarper if you adopt the man-eating Madonna approach.

The male species, you see, requires careful handling — although they can be all mouth and showy talk when they're careering around the place with the "lads", they can wither away to a mass of frazzled nerves in certain situations. Asking a girl out comes high on their pet fears list.

"Girls always expect boys to make the first move," says Stephen, who's 18. "They moan about having to hang around waiting to be asked out, but actually plucking up the courage and saying 'Will you go out with me?' is much worse. There's no rule to say that a girl shouldn't ask a boy out, but they rarely do. I only wish more of them were a bit more daring — it'd certainly make my life a lot easier!"

YOU have to admit that Stephen's got a point there. If the thought of asking a boy out turns you into a mass of quivering blancmange, why should it be any different for a boy? Practice doesn't seem to make it any easier. Stephen explains: "It wouldn't be so bad if girls gave you a bit of encouragement and made it slightly more obvious that they'd say yes. But you usually just have to take the chance."

Supposing, then, that tagging along hot on his heels has started to get a bit on the boring side. It's easy for friends to push you into asking him out — when it comes down to it, suggesting a date can be pretty nerve racking . . . but there are ways and means.

Don't forget that boys have the ability to turn deep pink to the ends of their earlobes too, especially when they're with mates and feel they've got a certain image to live up to. Barging in and singling him out from a huge group isn't a particularly good idea — the crowd will fall silent, everyone will turn and stare at your 'victim' (nudge, nudge, she fancies you, haw! haw! etc) and the chances are he'll bluff his way out of a tight spot with a few clumsy excuses. Getting him alone is, without a doubt, much more effective.

Asking a boy out needn't be a solemn occasion. In fact, spouting out a carefully worded sentence when you've barely passed the "hello" stage can make the whole thing seem like a bigger deal than it actually is. A casual approach is less nerve racking and a much more natural way of asking

someone out than blurting "Fancy a date?" out of the blue.

Say you've spotted him on his own. You don't have to be in the Lenny Henry league of wit to start a conversation, and wise-cracking conversation openers often backfire. Stick to the simple ones. "Wasn't maths awful today?" might sound awfully corny and un-funny (basically because it is), but you'll be less likely to scare the socks off him if you ease yourself into conversation gently. He'll reply and you can suggest a coffee after school to recover. As long as you keep it on an easy-going friendly basis, he shouldn't cringe at the thought.

THERE'S no guarantee, of course, that an innocent cup of coffee will lead to the sort of stuff that Barbara Cartlands' are made of. But at least you'll gradually begin to feel bolder, more relaxed and more able to talk to the man in question as a person rather than some god you've worshipped from afar since you were nine.

"But I couldn't possibly go up to him and ask him out, no matter how casual it sounds," you protest. So the very sight of him turns you to jelly and you know for sure that you'd turn scarlet as soon as you uttered your first word. So what? Turning a bit pink round the edges isn't the end of the world. It's a cliché, but blokes do find blushes attractive.

If all this sounds like a horrible dream that you couldn't possibly cope with, there's always the good old telephone. Some people do feel safer a couple of miles away on the other end of the line, and there's the advantage that you can loosely plan out (and even write down) what you're going to say before your quaking fingers actually dial the number.

A casual note is another idea, but letters can be interpreted in very different ways. It's a bit dramatic, too, the sort of thing that's likely to shock him into silence.

If you can handle it, go for the face-to-face approach. Pick a time when you're feeling confident, know you look good and don't forget that asking someone out is something that boys have to cope with all the time. As Stephen says, "If I really like a girl, I pluck up the courage to ask her out by telling myself that the worst that can happen is that she'll say no. So I've lost nothing by trying."

Instead of perching on the edge of your seat hoping that he'll amble over and ask you for a dance, why not make the move yourself? After all, there's a fifty-fifty chance he'll say, oooh yes please . . .!

SPO

A GOOD

SWIMMING

All you need is a costume that won't come apart in embarrassing places and a bath towel (a swimming pool might come in handy, too). If you're under sixteen you'll get a reduction in the price but they generally don't charge much anyway.

If you can't swim, most pools have special classes — it really is worth learning.

Swimming is one of the best sports for all-over fitness. It'll strengthen back and shoulder muscles.

30 mins. vigorous swimming uses up about 200 calories.

CYCLING

Get on yer bike (if you have one) and get out there. Get together with some mates and set off on a nice day. It's best to stick to quieter roads and it's not really much fun in the rain.

The good thing is that it doesn't cost you anything once you've got a bike, and if you haven't, look out for a good second-hand bargain in your local paper.

Cycling is especially good for calf and thigh muscles as well as aerobic fitness (lungs and heart).

30 minutes energetic cycling uses up about 125 calories.

TENNIS

This sport can work out a bit more expensive. A racket can cost anything from about £10 up. Some tennis clubs insist you have to wear white, so that can cost a fair bit too. Hiring a court is cheaper if four of you go and split it between you. You can play doubles or have a singles contest.

The only thing is that it's not very easy if you've never played before — you'd probably be better to have a couple of lessons.

It really builds up your arm muscles and your legs (because you spend half the time chasing the ball off the court!).

minutes tennis will burn up about 160 calories.

The good thing about this sport is that it can be played all year round because it's an indoor sport. Again you may need to buy a racket; that'll cost anything from £10 to £100. Leisure centres usually hire them out, though. You'll also need to pay to hire out a court.

You don't need so much strength in your arms for this, as for tennis. It'll make your wrists flexible and if it's a good game, you'll be running around a bit so it's good for all-over fitness.

30 minutes will burn up about 160 calories.

JOGGING

You really have to get proper running shoes if you don't want to damage your knees. A good pair cost from £20 up to about £60.

You don't really need a fancy jogging suit or anything but it might be useful. You certainly shouldn't wear anything tight.

Once you've bought the basics it doesn't cost anything, though.

Great for all-over fitness. Builds up your leg muscles and gets rid of that flab on your thighs!

30 minutes energetic jogging uses about 270 calories.

KEEP FIT AND AEROBICS

You can do this at home using the special tapes or records which is good if you're embarrassed about bouncing around in a leotard.

Otherwise most towns have classes. It's best to go to someone who's a qualified instructor — they'll make sure you do the exercises properly and don't hurt yourself.

Classes can be as cheap as 50p an hour. You might want to buy a leotard, so that could cost a bit, but otherwise anything loose and comfy will do.

Keep fit is less strenuous than aerobics, but both will tone up your muscles.

30 minutes uses up about 140 calories.

Lots of ideas to burn up those extra calories . . .

There're so many different sports around nowadays that there's bound to be something to suit you, your pocket and your lifestyle. Even if the thought of a lazy evening in front of the telly with your feet up and a packet of Maltesers at your elbow seems more inviting than a brisk three mile jog in the snow — it really is worth the effort, and yes, it can even be fun!

Here are some of the most popular sports, roughly how much they'll put you out of pocket and how much good they do you . . .

Once a year . . .

Spring is sprung.
Summer sizzles (if we're lucky!)
Autumn falls.
Christmas comes.
Boys do the washing up.
'Slade' get into the charts.
Everyone has a birthday (the Queen has
two . . .)
The Jackie office is cleaned up.
The News At Ten has good news.
Valentine's Day arrives and none of us
ever get cards (sniffle).
Some scientist pops up and tells us that
something we're eating is particularly bad
for us.
The 'Wizard of Oz' is on TV.
The Queen makes a speech.
The Ed. doesn't shout at us for being late.
Terry Wogan DOESN'T appear on TV.
We get a day off (or is that every two
years?)
YOU GET YOUR JACKIE ANNUAL!

ANNUAL CELEBRATIONS

August Bank Holiday

The day when the ancient tradition of traf-ick-jams is observed. All car owners stop working for one Monday a year , drive their vehicles on to the nearest motorway and stay there all day.

The Superbowl

This was once only celebrated in the New World but modern techniques have brought it to the civilised world.

Crowds of people gather round colour TV apparatuses and consume vast amounts of American beer and popcorn and shout loudly. A tolerance for ad. breaks every 30 seconds is an advantage.

The Annual England/ Scotland Football Match

The outcome of which decides the mood of an entire country for a whole day.

Burns Night

The object of the evening is to get someone to eat haggis and then tell them what it's made of.

January Sales

This is where hundreds of people get up at the crack of dawn and fight with each other to buy something they wouldn't be seen dead in because there's £20 off the price.

Saints' Days

On March 1st, St David's day, everyone in Wales wanders around with leeks (the vegetable type) in their lapels!

Just when they're getting over the excitement, the Irish start hunting for four-leafed shamrocks for St Patrick's Day, March 17th.

Then on April 23rd, St George's Day, good old-fashioned English heroes go out in search of the odd dragon and of course the Scots find ANOTHER excuse to get drunk at the end of the year when they celebrate St Andrew's Day on November 30th.

ONCE A YEAR. . . STEVE! (*FAN CLUB ED!*)

Steve stops talking.
Steve has a bath.
Steve buys cream cakes.
Steve opens his wallet.
Steve gets a haircut.
Steve wins at pool against Mike.
Steve buys new shoes.
Steve changes his socks.
Steve works.
Steve and Cathy call a truce.
Steve receives a fan letter.
Steve gets *very* angry indeed with all the insults . . .

ONCE A YEAR. . . MIKE! (*FEATURES ED!*)

Mike arrives on time.
Mike wears an ironed shirt.
Mike shaves.
Mike loses at pool against Steve.

Christmas Comes But Once A Year

The Christmas tree was believed to have been invented by a pretty clever chap called Martin Luther. The story goes that old Mart' was walking home one night when he saw the stars reflecting off the branches of a tree! So moved by it was he, that when he got home, he then had the really wacky idea of putting candles on a tree in his living room.

1843 saw the first ever Christmas card.

1955 saw Dickie Valentine's 'Christmas Alphabet' become the very first Christmas number one.

Legend has it that the largest cracker ever produced was 45 feet long and 8 feet wide!

KUNG HEI FAT CHOY! (*It means "Happy New Year" in Chinese*).

February 9th at 12.00 midnight the corks fly and masses of sweet and sour balls are consumed as the Chinese celebrate their New Year. 1986, according to them, was the "Year of the Tiger" and 1987, "The Year of the Cat" (sounds like there's a song in there).

To find out whether you're a rat, cat or even a monkey, check our chart.

1964	Dragon
1965	Snake
1966	Horse
1967	Goat
1968	Monkey
1969	Rooster
1970	Dog
1971	Pig
1972	Rat
1973	Buffalo
1974	Tiger
1975	Cat
1976	Dragon

BIRTHDAY TRIVIA

● *Kenny Everett was born on Christmas Day.*
● *Mario Andretti, the racing driver, won the World Grand Prix Championship in 1978 at the tender age of 9 — he was born on February 29, 1940.*
● *More people are born between March and May than in any other period. The fewest birthdays occur in November.*
● *Rowan Atkinson, Sacha Distel, Joan of Arc and Richard II were all born on January 6.*
● *George Michael shares his birthday with General Custer and a writer named William Smellie. Says it all, really, doesn't it . . .?*
● *Stephen "Duff Duff" Tinny was born on the day King Arthur and Joan of Arc died. Someone tried to kill Queen Victoria on this date (May 30) but it didn't quite come off.*
● *Paul Weller was born on May 25 — the same day on which, in 1885, the Oxford boat crew rowed from Dover to Calais in 4½ hours.*
● *David Bowie and Shirley Bassey were both born on January 8th.*
● *Tom Bailey was born on the day Captain Scott reached the South Pole — give or take a few years.*
● *On Lloyd Cole's birthday, January the 31st, over 250 people fell into canals in Amsterdam and drowned in 1790 because it was so foggy. The conspirators in the Gunpowder Plot were also executed on this day in 1606. Question — which of these events was the least disastrous?*
● *Neil Kinnock, Michael Parkinson and Dirk Bogarde (who?) all share the same birthday.*

LAST CHRISTMAS

IT WAS NEW YEAR'S EVE . . .

YOUR MUM AND I HAVE BEEN TALKING, MOIRA. WE'VE DECIDED NOT TO GO OUT TONIGHT. WE DON'T THINK YOU SHOULD BE HERE ALONE, AFTER THOSE CARDS YOU GOT.

DON'T BE SILLY, DAD. WE ALL MADE OUR PLANS FOR NEW YEAR AGES AGO.

YOU AND MUM JUST GO AHEAD. BESIDES, AUNT BETTY'LL BE DISAPPOINTED IF YOU DON'T.

BUT WE DON'T WANT YOU TO BE ON YOUR OWN, DEAR.

I WON'T BE ON MY OWN. COLIN'LL BE BACK FROM CORNWALL IN TIME FOR NEW YEAR, AND SUZY'S COMING ROUND EARLY TO HELP ME GET THINGS READY FOR THE PARTY. I'D RATHER YOU WENT AHEAD WITH YOUR PLANS, HONESTLY.

WELL . . . IF YOU'RE SURE, DEAR . . .

I'LL FEEL A LOT BETTER ONCE COLIN GETS HERE. HE SAID HE'D TRY TO ARRIVE A COUPLE OF HOURS BEFORE THE PARTY . . .

BUT A LITTLE LATER THERE WAS A PHONE CALL . . .

HELLO, MOIRA? IT'S COLIN. LISTEN, I'M IN A PHONE BOX MILES FROM NOWHERE. I'VE BEEN TRYING TO DRIVE UP, BUT A LOT OF THE ROADS ARE BLOCKED. I DON'T THINK I'LL MAKE IT BY MIDNIGHT.

OH . . . WELL . . . IT — IT CAN'T BE HELPED. I'LL SEE YOU WHEN I SEE YOU, THEN.

IS ANYTHING WRONG, LOVE? YOU SOUND WORRIED ABOUT SOMETHING.

NO, I — I'M FINE, COLIN. JUST TAKE CARE ON THE ROADS, OK?

OH, COLIN . . . I REALLY WANTED YOU TO BE HERE. BUT I — I'D BETTER NOT TELL MUM AND DAD, OR THEY MIGHT START WORRYING AND CHANGE THEIR PLANS AGAIN . . .

AND, A COUPLE OF HOURS LATER . . .

WELL, YOU TWO CAN GET OFF TO AUNT BETTY'S NOW SUZY'S HERE. HAVE A GOOD TIME.

ALL RIGHT, DEAR. I FEEL BETTER KNOWING SUZY AND COLIN ARE GOING TO BE HERE WITH YOU.

WHEN'LL COLIN BE ARRIVING?

HE — HE WON'T BE. NOT BEFORE WE SEE THE NEW YEAR IN, ANYWAY. HE'S BEEN HELD UP. I JUST DIDN'T WANT TO TELL MUM AND DAD THAT.

ARE YOU STILL THINKING ABOUT THOSE CARDS FROM DEREK?

YES. I — I JUST DON'T KNOW WHAT'S HAPPENING TO ME, SUZY. IT IS DEREK'S HANDWRITING THAT'S ON THEM. AND I'M SURE THE RING THAT CAME WITH THE SECOND CARD IS HIS . . .

I KEEP THINKING OF LAST NEW YEAR'S EVE. WHEN I HAD THAT TERRIBLE FIGHT WITH HIM AT YOUR PARTY. IT WAS THE LAST TIME I EVER SAW HIM ALIVE . . . EXACTLY A YEAR AGO TONIGHT . . .

I TRIED TO CONCENTRATE ON PREPARING FOR THE PARTY . . .

OH, THAT'S THE PHONE. COULD YOU GET IT, SUZY? I'VE GOT COTTAGE CHEESE ALL OVER MY FINGERS!

AND . . .

WHAT IS IT, SUZY? YOU LOOK LIKE SOMETHING'S SCARED YOU! WH — WHO WAS IT ON THE PHONE?

MOIRA . . . IT — IT SOUNDED . . . IT SOUNDED LIKE DEREK'S VOICE! I KNOW IT'S IMPOSSIBLE, BUT I'D SWEAR IT WAS HIM . . .

HE SAID HE WANTED TO REMIND YOU HE'LL BE COMING TO THE PARTY TONIGHT. HE — HE'LL ARRIVE AT MIDNIGHT, HE SAID . . . JUST AS THE NEW YEAR IS STRIKING . . .

OH NO!

I FEEL LIKE I'M GOING CRAZY! HOW CAN ANY OF THIS BE HAPPENING?

THE OTHER GUESTS ARRIVED . . . AND THE OLD YEAR CREPT TOWARDS ITS END . . .

WHAT'S GOING TO HAPPEN WHEN MIDNIGHT STRIKES? I — I DON'T THINK I CAN BEAR TO WAIT HERE IN THE HOUSE TO FIND OUT . . .

I — I'M THE ONE DEREK'S COMING FOR . . . I'VE GOT TO GET AWAY FROM HERE!

BUT AS MOIRA TRIED TO RUN OUT OF THE HOUSE . . .

NO! L-LET ME GO!

IT'S JUST ME, LOVE. WHAT'RE YOU RUNNING AWAY FOR? THE PARTY ISN'T THAT BAD, IS IT?

COLIN! OH, THANK GOODNESS!

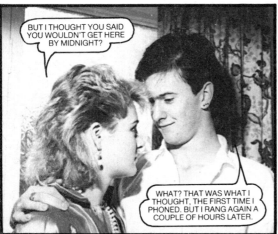

BUT I THOUGHT YOU SAID YOU WOULDN'T GET HERE BY MIDNIGHT?

WHAT? THAT WAS WHAT I THOUGHT, THE FIRST TIME I PHONED. BUT I RANG AGAIN A COUPLE OF HOURS LATER.

IT WAS SUZY WHO TOOK THE CALL. DIDN'T SHE TELL YOU?

OH . . . NO, I — I'M SORRY, I FORGOT . . .

BUT YOU ONLY ANSWERED THE PHONE ONCE TONIGHT, SUZY . . . AND YOU SAID IT WAS DEREK'S VOICE YOU'D HEARD!

I — I DON'T UNDERSTAND, SUZY. DID YOU JUST MAKE IT UP ABOUT THE PHONE CALL, TO SCARE ME?

NO . . . OF — OF COURSE I DIDN'T . . .

WILL SOMEBODY PLEASE TELL ME WHAT'S GOING ON?

SO . . .

YOU SAY YOU FINALLY BROKE UP WITH DEREK AT THE NEW YEAR PARTY LAST YEAR, MOIRA? WHOSE HOUSE WAS THE PARTY AT?

SUZY'S PLACE. ALL THE GANG WERE INVITED THERE.

THAT'S WHAT I THOUGHT. YOU SEE, YOU'RE PROBABLY RIGHT ABOUT IT BEING DEREK'S HANDWRITING ON THESE CARDS . . . BUT HE WROTE THEM A YEAR AGO, BEFORE THE ACCIDENT . . .

I'LL BET THIS IS THE CARD SUZY GOT FROM DEREK LAST YEAR . . . AND THE GIFT CARD WAS WITH WHATEVER HE SENT HER. DON'T YOU SEE? IT SAYS 'I'LL SEE YOU AT YOUR NEW YEAR'S EVE PARTY' . . .

YOU MEAN . . . HE MEANT SUZY'S PARTY?

IS IT TRUE, SUZY? DID YOU KEEP THE CARDS YOU GOT FROM DEREK LAST CHRISTMAS . . . AND THEN SEND THEM TO ME THIS YEAR, TO MAKE ME THINK THEY'D COME FROM HIM?

YES! AND IT REALLY SCARED YOU, DIDN'T IT?

BUT WHY?

I — I LOVED DEREK. NEITHER OF YOU EVER KNEW THAT, DID YOU? I ALWAYS LOVED HIM . . . AND IT WAS YOUR FAULT HE DIED! IF YOU HADN'T SPLIT UP WITH HIM LAST NEW YEAR HE MIGHT NOT HAVE DRIVEN OFF LIKE THAT . . . HE MIGHT STILL BE ALIVE!

THAT ISN'T TRUE, SUZY. DEREK'S DEATH WAS AN ACCIDENT!

LET HER GO, MOIRA. THERE'S NO POINT TRYING TO REASON WITH HER NOW.

SHE WANTED TO FRIGHTEN YOU, AS SOME SORT OF REVENGE FOR WHAT SHE THOUGHT YOU'D DONE TO DEREK. IT WOULD BE EASY ENOUGH TO GET HOLD OF A RING THAT LOOKED LIKE HIS AND SEND IT WITH THAT CARD.

WE'D NEVER EVEN HAVE GUESSED, IF SHE HADN'T LIED ABOUT YOUR PHONE CALL . . .

IT'S OVER NOW, ANYWAY . . . HEY, LOOK AT THE TIME! IT'S MIDNIGHT!

YES . . . THE START OF A NEW YEAR . . .

AND THE END OF A NIGHTMARE . . .

THE END

"COME NUMBER FOUR!"

THE pile of blankets in the corner of the porch lifted and scared the living daylights out of me.

I threw down the Sunday papers and screamed!

A bleary-eyed face surfaced from the mess of material.

"What time is it?"

My jaw dropped. His hair was blond and crumpled, his eyelids drooping over liquid eyes.

"It must be early," he said. "Break it to me gently."

"It's after seven," I said and the boy exhaled and ran his fingers through his haystack hair.

"Well," I said and tipped my check peaked cap, "almost."

"Are you a burglar?"

"Don't be silly," I said. "I'm the paper-girl."

"Amazing," he muttered.

He groaned as I backed out of the porch door, hefted my bag and retreated down the path. The boy in the porch had given me a jolt.

He must have been locked out. Why else bed down in the porch? No doubt his parents were keen on curfews — like mine. I risked an inquisition each time I ventured out.

"Where are you going?"

"Who with?"

"What time will you be back?"

"Oh Mum!"

"Claudia, now listen, your father will be round at Pam's at eleven, he'll wait for you."

We argued, I sulked and conversation was reduced to a minimum. They cut my pocket money, and I defiantly started my paper-round as an economic alternative.

They took it reasonably well — apart from a moan about my jolting them awake in the morning as I stumbled about in the half-light before setting off for the paper shop where Frank dispensed the marked-up rounds with the discipline of a sergeant-major.

It was a couple of days after my porch episode and I was lounging against the shop window when Frank barked out, "Number four!"

I marched straight in. Frank plonked the pile of papers in front of me and I began shovelling them into my dayglo bag.

"Any extras?" I said.

"Nope."

"Any off?"

"Nope."

Frank was a man who believed in word rationing and I shouldered the news before making for the door. His unexpected voice halted me in my tracks.

"Some boy with a corn stook instead of hair has been asking for you."

"That so?" I asked, trying to appear dead casual.

"Call her number four, I said."

Frank's granite face softened.

"Thanks Frank," I said. The porch-boy, looking for me!

"I was going to ask you to stay out late . . ."

All week I attacked my round zealously, but each time I drew a blank at his door.

On Saturday, when I was fitting the local paper into the letterbox, the door opened.

● *Specially written for Jackie by Sam White*

"Number four?"

He stood with the night in his face and handsomely dishevelled.

"Most people call me Claudia."

"Understood," he said. "How do you manage to get up this early every day?"

"It's easy," I said and felt a surge of affection. "I go to bed early."

"Pity," he said. "I was going to ask you to stay out late."

His smile egged me on.

"I AM allowed out after dark," I considered.

"Could you come?" he asked.

"Name a day."

"Tonight?"

"Love to," I said. "Outside the paper-shop?"

"Perfect," he said.

"I was going to say the same," I said, wondering how on earth I was going to obtain a late night pass.

EACH time I summoned up the courage to ask Mum and Dad, some obstacle blocked my run-up.

Finally, I leap-frogged the whole thing by announcing at eight-thirty I was going to bed early.

I raced upstairs, stuffed a few pillows down my bed in an effigy of a body, crept back downstairs, sneaked out of the front door and tip-toed off down the road.

"Hi," said Rob, stepping out from the shadow of the paper-shop entrance. "Glad you could make it."

I don't think I'd ever been taken out by somebody as entertaining as Rob. First we went to a hamburger place with real style and the right flavour music, and deeper into the night it was a haunt where the customers clustered at circular tables round a circular stage.

At twelve a magician appeared to perform the trickiest feats of magic, including the apparent dismemberment of a volunteer from the audience.

"Surely she was in the know," I said.

"Apparently not," said Rob as we watched the restored lady return to her relieved boyfriend.

I was under Rob's spell and when the band struck up a tune he took me out on to the floor and as we circled I laid my head on his shoulder and blessed my paper-round.

I slipped back home at three with his goodnight kiss burning on my cheek. But it seemed I'd only just sneaked between the sheets when the jangling alarm attacked me at six. I winched myself out of bed and staggered around for my clothes.

Frank said I looked like something the sea had washed up, and I felt pretty light-headed as I began stabbing papers into the letterboxes.

I livened right up at Rob's house. There he was crumpled against the door — fast asleep. I watched him for a moment and my heart went out to him.

"Hey, sleepy," I said. "Wake up."

His eyes winched open as if weights were strapped to the lids.

"Am I dreaming?" he said with the daylight creasing his face.

"You got locked out?"

"It's a habit, the parents won't trust me with a key."

"At least they let you stay out late," I said.

"We argue a lot."

"I've given up speaking to mine!"

"We're misunderstood," he said and we each aired our ills until Rob grabbed his parents, paper and created a terrible racket jamming it through the door.

"I can blame the paper-girl for waking them up," he said and laughed as I punched him in retaliation.

My honeymoon period with Rob lasted about two dates. Another of my stop-outs with the pillows decoy in the bed and I was rumbled by Mum on one of her night patrols.

When I attempted my low profile return I was confronted by both my parents.

"Claudia," said Dad, "what's going on?"

"I suppose this boy is the usual no-hoper?"

"I was just a little late, Dad, that's all," I said and tried to sneak off to bed.

"I wondered why you were looking so tired," said Mum, grabbing my sleeve as I tried to duck past.

"I suppose this boy is the usual no-hoper?"

"No he's not," I said. "He's like me."

"You're to be in by nine for a week," said Dad.

"Worse than prison," I muttered.

"Don't be so rude!"

I stomped to my bedroom and battered my pillow with exasperation. It was so unfair.

I met him at the weekend. We idled round the shops and in the plaza sat close on the bench watching a busker play his tunes.

I SIGHED and reached for Rob's hand. He threaded his fingers through mine.

"My parents think you're a bad influence," I said. "Tempting me out late."

"I was born for the night," he said and swamped me with his eyes.

"Oh Rob," I said and weakened as he swooped in to kiss me.

I arrived home with an hour to spare. Rob had seemed fidgety and keen to be away, and when I awoke with the dawn I felt low.

It was overcast and grey when I wandered down to the paper-shop. There were the usual figures clustered under the awning and I signalled to all the ones I knew. We danced on the spot to keep warm.

Frank was bellowing, "Number two!"

Little Keith pushed through the glass door and picked up his round.

"Number three!"

Frank's voice boomed out yet again and we all glanced at one another.

"Where's Paul?" said somebody.

"He's left," said another.

"What?" I said. There was a sudden blur of orange as somebody crashed through the door to emerge a minute later with an untidy bundle of papers jutting from their bag.

"Rob!"

"This is a nightmare, Claudia," he said and swayed to a halt.

I laughed. I was so happy. There was Rob — tousled and tired but with a grin on his face.

"I did it for you," he said and much to the surprise of everyone I marched straight up and planted a smacker on his lips.

"Number four!" shouted Frank.

Do you chatter too much? Our quiz finds out your rabbit rating!

talk talk

What happens when you enter a room? Do people flock round you, do they start to yawn, or do they all get up and leave? In other words, do you talk too much? Read on . . .

1. When you get up in the morning, what are your first words likely to be?
a) "Umph, uuuuurghhh . . ."
b) "Morning. Wassatime?"
c) "Morning, everyone! What a marvellous morning! What are we going to do today?"

2. When you meet a friend you haven't seen for ages, do you:
a) natter on, and then realise you've not let her get a word in edgeways yet, and go all pink and foolish, and start asking her what SHE'S been doing?
b) feel pleased, and quite happy to listen to what she's got to say?
c) tell her what's been going on since you last met?

3. When you meet someone new, what do you do?
a) Tell them all about yourself.
b) Ask what they do and where they live and things.
c) Ask what they think about the area, and what they like doing, what sort of music they like, etc., and tell them what you like to do.

4. You're telling people about this amazing thing that happened to you. How are they reacting?
a) You're not quite sure, but they must be fascinated, as it *was* so amazing.
b) They're listening and asking questions, and it starts off a whole new discussion.
c) You've told them very briefly, so they won't get bored.

5. When you've told someone how to do something, what sort of thing do they say?
a) "Mmm, what was that?"
b) "Yes yes yes yes yes yes all RIGHT!"
c) "Yes, I see."

6. You've just been on the phone for half an hour to a friend. When Mum says "What's Anne been up to lately, then?"

do you reply:
a) "Oh, lots of things," and give her a condensed account?
b) "The usual, I suppose"?
c) "This 'n' that . . ."?

7. You're having a group discussion at school or work. What do you do?
a) Try to make yourself as inconspicuous as possible, in case you get asked a question.
b) Think of something to say, and keep on saying it so that no-one else gets a word in.
c) Listen carefully to what's been said and make a contribution if it's necessary, or if you're asked to.

8. When you're involved in a conversation with someone, do you:
a) think very carefully before saying anything, to make sure that it's an appropriate thing to say?
b) chat away to them, and listen to what they've got to say?
c) say lots of interesting things to entertain and impress them?

9. After an evening with friends, if you look back on it, what do you remember?
a) Lots of giggles, general friendly atmosphere, and chat.
b) Lots of things that people did and said.
c) Not a lot.

SCORING
1. a) 1, b) 2, c) 3. If you scored c) we're surprised no-one's murdered you yet!
2. a) 2 (Let's face it, we all do it!), b) 1, c) 3.
3. a) 3, b) 1 (Um, you tried, but this way you get answers like "Liverpool" and "I dig drains".) c) 2.
4. a) 3 (Try looking at them, and see if they really are fascinated.) b) 2, c) 1.
5. a) 1, b) 3, c) 2.
6. a) 2, b) 3, (If she'd just eloped with an oil sheik, would she have had the chance to tell you?) c) 1.
7. a) 1, b) 3, c) 2.
8. a) 1, b) 2, c) 3.
9. a) 2. Sounds great, can we come along too, sometime? b) 1, c) 3.

RESULTS
9-14: There's a lot to be said for being a good listener, but if you don't open your mouth occasionally people might not even realise you're there! The only way you get to know people and people get to know you is by talking to them. People won't know what a warm and witty person you are if you just sit there and say nothing — they're not mind-readers, you know! So switch on your brain, polish your tonsils, and talk!

15-21: Most of the time you're probably a good person to have a conversation with — a good talker and a good listener as well. We bet you're pretty popular, though you may be shy occasionally in unfamiliar company, and if you've got something that's very important to you on your mind you may go on a bit about it. But as long as you look out for the tell-tale signs of boredom, like glassy eyes, yawning, staring at the floor, etc., you should be OK.

22-27: If you don't cork up, you're in grave danger of being prosecuted by the RSPCH (Royal Society for Prevention of Cruelty to Humans). You open your mouth as soon as you get up, and that's it for the day (unless someone manages to shove a sock in it). It probably just rabbits on of its own accord after a bit, without you having much of a clue what it's on about. Haven't you noticed people running away shrieking (and probably jumping out of windows) as you approach? If you jabber on all the time as a result of nerves, here's a tip: relax, and listen to what the other person's saying occasionally! There's nothing wrong with an occasional gap in the conversation, so if you don't want to become a Bore, buy a guidebook to the human head, locate your ears, and switch them ON!

STEPPING OUT OR STAYING IN?

Saturday socialite or steady stay-at-home? We wondered what people did with their weekend and cornered some Saturday shoppers . . .

MARION ▲
"I'm going to a party tonight. I think I'll wear my green skirt which sort of wrinkles — it's slinky!"

▲ **KENNETH (left)**
"I'm just here for the day visiting George who's my cousin. I'm from Mallaig. When I get back tonight, it'll be too late to go out. I usually go to the disco in the community hall."

GEORGE ▲
"I'll be staying in tonight, I've got no money."

JOHN ▶
"You're not going to take photographs of me, are you? I haven't even spiked my hair today. I usually go dancing on a Saturday night in Struts disco in Barrowland. I like Gothic music by peole like the Sex Gang Children or The Cult. It takes me ages to get ready to go out."

ANNE-MARIE AND STEPHEN ▼
"Stephen works on a Saturday night so our big night for going out is Friday. We like to go to restaurants — especially to eat curries and Chinese food."

LORRAINE ▲
"I'm staying in tonight. I'm going to pamper myself — you know, wash my hair, put on a face mask, that sort of thing."

ALAN ▼
"I work on a Saturday, but since I can lie in on Sunday, I like to go out and enjoy myself on a Saturday night. I usually end up at a night club."

BILLY ▲
"I finish work at six o'clock and I'll probably go out with my pals. My girlfriend's going to a party but I can't go because I'm working until quite late and the party starts early. I'll probably be too tired when I finish work anyway."

THREE INTO T·O·N·E

MESSIN' AROUND

This look'll see you through everything from a game of footy in the park to an evening at the ice-rink with your new man. You don't have to stick to chain-store fashion shops, just invest in a few basics like leggings and turtlenecks and build up from there . . .

Big cardies — Look in Oxfam, jumble sales or the bottom of the family wardrobe for big, chunky cardies in bright primary colours. Better still, bribe mum to knit you one from scratch . . .

Sticky-out skirts — Rummage through the jumblies for wild 50's print skirts, or make your own from wacky curtain fabric . . .

Plimmies — Track down a pair of black school pumps in the Children's department of any good shoe shop, or head for the Men's department instead and pick yourself a pair of bright baseball boots.

Hats — Down to your nearest army and navy stores for a rake through the berets and baseball caps — they're well-cheap and well-trendy.

Scarves — Dear little tartan scarves and bright fluffy mohairs can be found for pennies if you tour the local charity shops.

Ribbons — Liven up winter hair with a handful of bright ribbons from a fabric shop or a haberdashers.

Baskets — Just about the trendiest thing to cart all your rubbish about this year is an old-fashioned basket! Hunt in junk shops for the sort with coloured straw flowers woven into the design. You can pick up real classics for under a quid.

What do you do when your wardrobe's almost as empty as your purse? When last year's lime green leggings have been relegated to the dog's basket and your beloved skinny-rib mini is serving out its twilight years as a wash-rag for the family car? Pawn your stamp collection, break open the piggy bank and read on for three complete looks that won't break the bank, won't upset the neighbours, and best of all, won't be out of fashion by this time next week.

DRESS REHEARSAL

The local disco sort of loses its appeal when you have to turn up for the 8th week running in the same old jeans and pully. Dig out some real party clothes for a change . . .

Party dresses — Well, they just don't make them like this any more, so hunt down some real 50's originals. Look for wild, squiggly prints, polka dots and flowers, or romantic taffeta and lace creations. Keep your eyes peeled in the local charity shops or find out about second hand fashion shops in your area. Good hunting grounds are Kensington Market, Camden Market and The King's Road in London, Afflecks Palace in Manchester, The Barras in Glasgow, and Mega Active and Oasis in Birmingham.

Tights — It's worth shelling out a bit extra on really posh, lacy tights — you can't go wearing American Tan with *this* look.

Shoes — Second-hand shoes aren't a good idea because they'll have moulded themselves to someone else's feet. If you do a bit of detective work you might track down a really old-fashioned shoe shop that still has old stocks of baby stilettos, or a second hand fashion shop with a stock of unworn 50's and 60's shoes. Otherwise, hunt for bridal shoes or ballet pumps for a special look.

Junk jewellery — ask your granny, ask your mum, or rummage through the local junk shops for tacky paste jewellery to pile on the glitz. You should be able to find yourself a whole treasure trove for a couple of quid.

Gloves — Head for old-fashioned department stores and pick yourself a pair of silky or lacy gloves.

Lace — Search for lace offcuts and remnants at local fabric shops. Wear them as shawls, ribbons or just pin them to your dress with brooches for extra decadence.

Bags — Tacky beaded bags are better than any old PVC clutch bag to stash your bus fares in. Charity shops are an endless source . . .

WELL-SUITED

Princess Di, eat your heart out. You don't have to be rich and famous to dress sharp — borrow your style from the past for an original, classic look.

Suits — Look out for original 40's and 50's suits with tailored jackets, nipped-in waists and boxy, padded shoulders, or tweedy 60's versions with short skirts and ¾ length sleeves. Charity shops sometimes have real bargains nestling away amongst the crimplene trouser suits, but second-hand fashion shops and markets are a better bet.

Belts — A broad, shiny patent leather belt to cinch in blouses and clingy pencil skirts can be your fashion trademark. They're reasonably priced at most chainstores and markets.

Blouses — Original lace, crepe and broderie anglaise blouses are still cheap and quite easy to find in charity shops, jumble sales and second hand fashion shops. They're really unusual and pretty and go beautifully with tight, curvy skirts.

Hats — Smart, sleek hats with dinky little veils, feathers, fruit or flowers are easily found and they add instant style. Spear with a hatpin for safety!

Handbags — Big, shiny old-fashioned handbags can be yours for a quiet word with any ageing auntie — great for hauling around your crepe scarves, 50's powder compacts, white gloves etc . . .

We fire 20 questions at Feargie.

ARE YOU BIG-HEADED?
Well, I can't get any hats to fit me!

WHAT WAS THE HAPPIEST MOMENT OF YOUR LIFE?
Being born!

DID YOU ENJOY YOUR CHILDHOOD?
Yes. I spent most of it dismantling my family's household things — fridges, cookers, washing-machines and so on — to try to find out how they worked. Trouble was, I could never work out how to get the things back together again! I had a happy childhood but it was misery for everyone else.

WHO IS THE MOST FAMOUS PERSON YOU'VE EVER MET?
Her name slips my mind!

WHICH IS YOUR FAVOURITE POP RECORD?
It would take me an hour to think of all of them.

WHICH IS YOUR MOST HATED POP RECORD?
And it would take me a year to think of all of THEM!

IF YOU COULD CHANGE ONE THING ABOUT YOUR APPEARANCE, WHAT WOULD IT BE?
My nose. It got broken while playing the Irish sport of hurling when I was a kid.

WHAT IS YOUR FAVOURITE COLOUR?
Black. Boring but it goes with everything.

QUESTION TIME WITH...

FEARGAL SHARKEY

DO YOU COLOUR YOUR HAIR?
No, it's NATURALLY yucky.

HAVE YOU EVER HIT ANYBODY?
If you dare to suggest that, I'll lay one on you!!!!

IF YOU WEREN'T A POP STAR, WHAT WOULD YOU LIKE TO DO?
I'd probably be a mad scientist and make robots or something!

HAVE YOU GOT A FAVOURITE FOOD?
Japanese raw fish. Pretty trendy, eh?

CAN YOU STAND ON YOUR HEAD?
No, my feet keep slipping off it.

DO YOU LIKE DRESSING UP?
In a word — YES. It's great to look good.

WHERE DO YOU GET YOUR STYLE?
You mean you think I've got style? At the moment, I'm wearing quite a lot of things from Comme des Garcons. But maybe tomorrow I'll just be wearing my tatty old jeans again!

WHAT IS YOUR HOBBY?
Destroying things. But seriously, I love all technology. Show me anything with wires and flashing lights and the first thing I want to do is to take a screw-driver to it and try to find out what makes it work.

WHAT'S THE FIRST THING YOU DO IN THE MORNING?
Try to forget about the silly things I did last night.

WHAT'S THE LAST THING YOU DO AT NIGHT?
Do some even sillier things than I did the night before!

WHAT WILL YOU BE DOING WHEN YOU ARE 65?
Trying to forget about all the incredibly silly things I did over the last sixty-five years.

ANY SPECIAL MESSAGE . . ?
If you can't join 'em, *beat 'em.*

here comes su

LOOK GOOD ALL SUMMER LONG . . .

TANNING TIPS

- Don't stay out in the sun too long too soon.
- Always use water-resistant lotions in or around water.
- Protect the most sensitive parts of your body — nose, shoulders, breasts, backs of knees — with a high protection factor or total block cream.
- Don't apply deodorant or perfume just before sunbathing.
- Protect your hair with a scarf or hat and never brush it when it's wet.
- Don't neglect after sun care. There's no point in getting a great tan if it all peels off the minute you get home. Use an after sun lotion to soften and smooth your skin after sunbathing.

COOL IT!

- Give your feet a squoosh of an aerosol foot freshener.
- Hold your wrists under cold running water.
- Wear loose cotton clothes rather than man-made fibres. Avoid tights in hot weather.
- Shower or bathe morning and evening.
- Use an effective anti-perspirant deodorant, except when sunbathing.
- Get rid of under-arm hair.

FEET FIRST!

- Put your best foot foward and treat yourself to a pedicure so you can go barefoot all summer long . . .
- Remove any old nail varnish and soak your feet in warm soapy water for about ten minutes then pat them dry.
- Trim toenails by cutting them straight across — don't cut the corners of the nails back into the nail grooves as they may lead to an ingrowing nail.
- Apply cuticle cream and gently push cuticles down with an orange stick wrapped in cotton wool. Finish off by rubbing in a little hand cream.

FACTOR FACTS

- What the sun tan filter factor system means . . .
2-3 For use on easily-tanned skin, not prone to burning, or when an initial tan has been established.
4-5 High protection to build up an initial tan on normal skin or for regular use on fair skin.
6-8 Ultra protection to protect very fair and sensitive skin prone to burning.
- Factor numbers are not yet standardised in Europe so you might find slight differences between different brands of suntan products.
Generally speaking Factor 5, for example, means that, without burning, you can stay in the sun five times longer than you can without protection.

EVERYTHING YOU'LL NEED ON YOUR HOLS

- There's no point in trying to cram your entire wardrobe into your suitcase for going off on holiday — whatever you may think, you won't wear half of it! Instead plan ahead, think of the type of holiday you're having — if you're rock-climbing for a fortnight in Wales there's need to pack bikinis and vest tops, is there???
- Here's a basic guide to what you'll ne for a beach type holiday . . .

Three pairs of shorts
Two cotton jumpers
Two skirts
Three vest dresses
As many T-shirts as you fancy
Cotton shirt
Ten pairs of knickers
Two bras (one strapless)
One pair of ankle socks
Bikini
Swimming costume
Beach towel
Sun tan lotion
After sun
Three different coloured belts
Plastic sandals
Flat pumps
Court shoes (for a night on the town)
Cotton wool
Skin cleanser, toner, moisturiser
Shampoo and conditioner
Hair gel and mousse
Toothbrush and toothpaste
Deodorant
Nail brush
Make-up remover
Sewing kit
First aid kit (Aspirins, sticking plaster, and something for an upset tummy)
Hairdryer
Travel adaptor
Travel wash, washing line, pegs
Coat hangers
Make-up bag
Camera
Personal stereo and tapes
Phrase book
Address book, pen
Sunglasses
Book

- And don't forget your passport, mone travellers' cheques and tickets!!!

mmer

.. AND THE
OFFICIAL STUFF!

As you know, if you're travelling
road, you'll need a passport.
plication forms for a ten-year United
gdom passport can be picked up at
ur local Post Office and state CLEARLY
w to go about applying for one.
member to post the application at least
r weeks before the date you travel. It
cost £15 and will last ten years if
u're over sixteen or five years if you're
der sixteen.

A British visitor's passport is valid for
e year and can be used for hols in most
untries in Europe. You can get this one
r the counter at the Post Office by
ng in an application form and
plying two passport photographs and
of of your identity. (Usually your birth
tificate). This one costs £7.50.

Remember to order your travellers'
ques and foreign money from your
nk about a week before your holiday.

's well worth taking out travel
urance wherever you're travelling, just
ase anything goes wrong! If you're
oking a package holiday you'll
bably be asked to take out insurance
the company, but if you're not sure
your travel agent to recommend a
d insurance company to you.
eck with your doctor eight to ten weeks
ore you travel whether or not you'll
d to be vaccinated against certain
eases. Don't panic — if you're
elling to Europe, chances are there'll
no problems, but if you're heading for
tic locations it's well worth having an
ction.

"glove story an

Put your best foot forward and have a glovely time!

Socks from a selection by The Sock Shop and Carolynne Read.

Gloves from a selection by Dents, Carolynne Read and The Sock Shop.

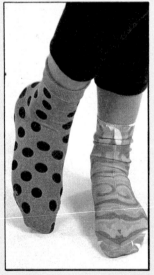

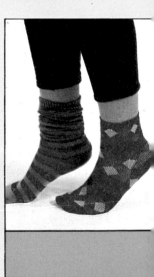

socks appeal"

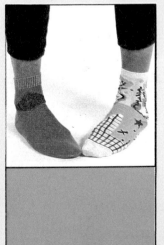

TWICE AS NICE!

. . . especially when the make-up is produced without cruelty to animals. We showed sisters Lynne and Gail how to make themselves up the natural way . . .

Lynne before

Gail before

Lynne gets the brush-off!

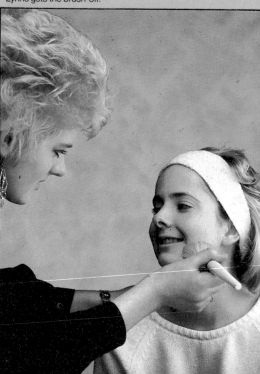

LYNNE Age 15
Make-up artist — Aileen

Aileen chose 'Ash Beige' foundati plus a medium cover-up stick to conceal any dark circles under the ey and the odd spot or blemish. She the applied 'Translucent' loose face powder with cotton wool and dusted off any excess with a big soft blusher brush.

For eyes Aileen picked 'Golden Oriole', a gold eyeshadow which she applied over the lid. Along the socket line she applied a medium brown shadow called 'Ginger Cat' followed b 'Timber Wolf', a dark brown on the outer edge. Aileen then accentuated the eyes with a brown kohl pencil and black mascara.

Blusher was the next stage — Aileen applied it after the eyeshadow so she could balance up the depth of colour. She chose 'Hot Chestnut' for the hollows of the cheeks and 'Shimmer' highlighter on the cheekbones.

For the final touch 'Topaz' lip colo was used on lips.

GAIL
Age 13
Make-up artist — Wendy

As Lynne and Gail have similar complexions Wendy opted for the same foundation, cover-up stick and powder.

For eyes she chose more of a pinky theme — 'Mink Wink', a cream shadow over the lid; 'Flamingo Flirt', a dusky pink on socket line and a plum shade called 'Barracuda' on the outer edge. Again the eyes were finished off with a brown kohl pencil and black mascara.

Finally, Wendy used 'Flamingo Flirt' eyeshadow as a blusher and 'Shimmer' highlighter followed by 'Sugar Plum' on the lips.

All make-up used was by Beauty Without Cruelty available from BWC stockists and health shops throughout the country.

Gail — beginning to blush!

The finished result!

LIVING BY
NUMBERS

*The Jackie staff, all clamouring to get a job
on Blue Peter, provide you with a number of things to
make (all without the use of sticky backed plastic.)*

NUMBER-SHAPED CUSHIONS

You'll need:
½ metre lining satin per cushion
Squared pattern paper (3 sheets)
2 bags of stuffing (for the 3 cushions)
2 metres braid for No. 2 cushion

First draw out your number on squared pattern paper.
Remember to add 1 cm. all round for the seam
allowance. Fold over the fabric, pin it to the paper and
cut out your number shapes.
Now is the time to decorate the cushions:
No. 1 cushion has small 1's stitched onto the front. To
do this draw the 1's on squared pattern paper and cut
out as many as you need. Pin them on to the right side
one piece of the cushion and sew into place using a
zig-zag stitch on a sewing machine.
No. 2 cushion is decorated with a double row of braid.
Pin the braid into place and sew on by hand.
No. 0 cushion has squiggly lines in contrasting thread
on its front. These are achieved by using the zig-zag
stitch on a sewing machine and sewing lines all over the
front of the cushion.

Having done this put the right sides of each cushion
together and sew up the seams. With the No. 0 it will be
necessary to cut the cushion as shown, otherwise it will
be impossible to turn it inside out properly. With all the
cushions remember to leave a gap to insert the stuffing.

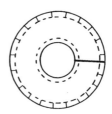

Turn the cushions inside ou
so that the right (decorated
sides are showing. Stuff
firmly and sew up the gaps

Cut on solid line.
Sew on dotted line.
Make small snips from cut,
curved edge, to the sewing
edge, to help when turning
inside-out.

SHOES

For the white plimsolls you'll need:
1 pair white plimsolls
1 jar of Dylon Colour-fun Fabric Paint
1 black felt-tipped pen

The digital-style numbers were simply
drawn on using a black felt-tipped pen.
Then paint round the sides of the shoes
and over the toecaps with Colour-fun
Fabric Paint.

For the black plimsolls you'll need:
1 pair black plimsolls
Scraps of coloured lining satin
Squared pattern paper

For each plimsoll cut out 1 large and 6
small numbers, first drawing your
pattern on squared pattern paper.
Simply sew these on to your shoe.

EWELLERY

r the Glittery Jewellery you'll need:
)acket of Fimo modelling material
assortment of tiny pearls, pieces of diamante, beads, etc
)acket of glitter
cm. of stiffish, coloured wire
cm. of the same wire
safety pin or brooch pin
cm. of thin copper wire
)air earring hooks
stud earring attachments (1 pair)

Fimo is a modelling material which is baked in the oven to harden it. First heat your oven to a temperature of 130°C. Place the jewellery on to a baking sheet and bake for approximately 30 mins. Take out and leave to cool.

sing a rolling pin on a wooden board, roll out the Fimo to a thickness of proximately half a centimetre. Out of this cut your number shapes, an 8 for the ndant, 1's for the earrings and a 6 for the brooch.

obtain the glittery effect press the small pearls, beads, diamantes etc *firmly* into e numbers on one side. When you have completed this, sprinkle glitter all over e number, press it on and shake off excess. If you are using a special brooch pin r the brooch, push this into the Fimo at the back of the brooch. Do the same with e earring studs if used, then bake as directed.

---

r the round Earrings you'll ed:
)acket of red and 1 of blue mo
)air earring wires
)air earring hooks

ll the red and blue Fimo out before and, from one colour, it circles. (I cut them round a piece). Using the other lour, cut out No. 1's and ess them into the circles king care that they keep their ape. Push earring wires into e top of each earring and ke in the oven till set. When ey are cool make loops from e earring wires, cutting off cess wire and insert hooks. ese can also be made as d earrings by pushing the ds into the back of the Fimo fore baking.

To make the necklace, take about 60 cm. of stiff wire, we found some pink electrical wire that matched the pendant. This was twisted round a pencil and pulled out to get a coiled effect. 5 cm. of thin copper wire was wound round the top of the 8 and this was then attached to the necklace wire. To fasten, simply twist the two ends of wire together at the back.

If you are using earring hooks for the earrings, first twist loops of thin copper wire round the top of each earring. You can attach the hooks to this. If you are not using a brooch pin for the brooch, first twist the 20 cm. of stiff wire round the brooch. A safety pin can be attached to the back of this and fastened under your clothes so that it doesn't show.

T-SHIRTS

For the printed T-shirt you'll need:
1 old, long-sleeved T-shirt
1 packet of Dylon Dye (Kingfisher, machine dye)
1 bottle of black and one of white Dylon Colour-fun fabric dye

The T-shirt was originally a wishy-washy pale green colour so it was first dyed Kingfisher according to the instructions on the packet. When dry it was simply painted with black No. 3's and white lines, using the fabric paint. To set the paint, press the dried garment under a cloth using a hot iron.

For the cut-out T-shirt you'll need:
1 short-sleeved T-shirt
2 packets of Dylon Dye
1 piece of squared pattern paper

The bottom was cut off the T-shirt to make a cropped top and the edges were hemmed. The top and bottom halves were then dyed contrasting colours.

On squared pattern paper draw out the numbers you wish to feature on your T-shirt. Pin these onto the top half of the T-shirt and cut round them. Cut squares out of the bottom half of the T-shirt and pin these onto the inside of the top half, making sure they cover the number-shaped holes. Sew into place using the zig-zag stitch on a sewing machine.

Michael J. Fox is ▷ just *so* cute! ▷

▽ OK, don't get too excited,
▽ here's Richard Gere, one
▽ of America's hottest
   sex symbols . . . Cor!

HUNKS!

JUST FEAST YOUR EYES ON THIS LOT!

Mel Gibson, smouldering ▷
as only he can do — just ▷
look at those eyes!

James Dean — the scowling hero without a cause, displaying those special qualities that set him apart from the rest!

◁ Sting's watching you, watching him, watching you . . .!

△ Beefcake Bruce Springsteen
△ flexes his muscles . . .

△ Here's Ali Campbell, lead singer of UB40.
Don't be deceived — he's not half as
△ innocent as he looks!

79

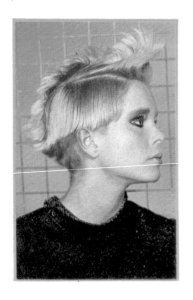

Jalle's clothes (including the silver **platforms**) are all second-hand. He got his braces from a selection at Kensington market.

Trine's **top** is from a jumble sale. **Skirt** was made from a pair of Levi's Jeans. **Tights** from Mary Quant. **Denim** platform shoes from a boot sale (in Brighton!) £2.50.

Jalle's denim **jacket** is self-customised and his **top** and **jeans** are both from a second-hand market.

Trine wears a cut-off **vest** from Marks and Sparks. Denim **skirt** is her own. Her **tights** are by Mary Quant.

glam rap!
Throw on the glitz and glam it up

Green **jacket** was picked up second-hand. Levi's **jeans** are Jalle's. **D.M.s** from Shelly's Shoes, 159 Oxford Street, London; £18.99.

'EastEnders V Corrie"

THE LADS

Wicksie: What more could a gal ask for than to snuggle down in Wicksie's motor, some soulful smoocheroonis on the cassette, and have the cheeky EastEnder whisper sweet naughties in your ear?

The Square's snappiest dresser is currently one of the most desirable objects in the soap scene. On a 'Whey Hey' rating of 1-10, Wicksie comes out with a massive *8.5.*

Kevin Webster: Working in a garage and buying his clothes from Top Man, Kev is yer typical lad! It wouldn't exactly be sweet and soulful with him, more a quick snog in the garage after hours.

He can be romantic if he tries, though, and one flash of that little boy in a man's world expression and you're hooked. If he combed his hair, and borrowed a decent shirt he might just make *6.*

Angie: Never mind the battle of the barmaids, there ain't *nobody* in soap-land who can touch old Ange. She drives the fellas barmy every time she shows her face (or more) and there can't be many of us around who haven't shed a tear for the poor girl.

She's not had what you'd call the best love life in the world and anyone who can spend so many years with Dirty Dennis deserves a medal, never mind The Jackie Annual Award for the most wonderful person in the whole of TV. No doubt about it, a maximum of *10.*

THE BARMAIDS

Bet: It's easy. While Angie has smudged much mascara over Dirty Den, Bet has had her own problems with dastardly Des Foster and a cast of thousands. While Angie isn't what you'd call subtle, Bet has the fashion sense of Sigue Sigue Sputnik, and it's not just the clothes, is it? Are we talking earrings or are we talking earrings?

Still, she does try and when it comes to put downs, Bet has the monopoly. A brave attempt by Miss Lynch, *7.*

THE BAD BOYS

Den: When it comes to being bad, Dennis grabs front page headlines every time he forgets to take Roly for a walk. He's the sort of chap your mum would dye her hair for, and go on, admit it, you wouldn't mind swapping your Michael J. Fox pillowcase for one of Dirty Den, would you?

More evil than Mavis Riley, this man has broken more hearts than Percy Sugden, no less than *8.*

Mike: The man behind Baldwin's Casuals (!) first gained his status as a bad boy by getting up to naughties with half the Barlows. "This man is a curse on my family," sobbed cuddly Ken. And it seems that every time he gets out of bed on the wrong side Mike takes it out on Ivy and the gals!

He's probably the nastiest thing you're likely to see in the Street but he's not really a patch on Dennis, *4.*

Lofty: This boy is just crying out to be mothered . . . or should that read smothered? There's never been a wally like this ever — no, not even Steven Wimp Wimp Duffy. Loft can't dress, can't think straight, can't see straight and can't even keep his room tidy. Would you marry this man???

A bit too unbelievable to be a real person, but everybody's somebody's baby and I suppose Lofty must have been at one time. He should try to learn a bit from Wicksie. A no-no, *3.*

WALLIES

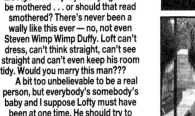

Curly: While Lofty has no brains, Curly overdoses on them, making him possibly the most boring person in the whole street. And I fear for anyone who spends most of their nights with Emily Bishop. One thing he does share with Lofty is looks and dress sense . . . who knows, they might even be brothers without knowing it?

The best thing that could happen to Curly would be for Bet Lynch to take him under her wing and teach him a few things about life. Until then I'm afraid it's a *5.*

CLEANERS

Ethel: Could anyone really be as dim as Ethel? (Who said John Taylor?) Rarely seen without her little Willie, she's become more of a good laugh than anything else. Likes a good gossip but generally gets the story wrong.

Winner of the worst wig in the world, Ethel's getting on a bit, but not really in Hilda's class. *4* out of 10, and *2* of that's for Willie!

Hilda: What can we say? Mention Coronation Street and people will immediately think Hilda Ogden. Gossip of the first class. If you want a story to get round, forget the front page of The Sun and just tell Hilda instead. If Angie had a mouth like hers she could get the whole chemist's down it, not just one bottle of pills. The pinnie, the lipstick, the curlers . . . what a woman: *10* out of 10.

EASTENDERS 33.5　　　　**CORONATION STREET 32**

shac

HOW TO KEEP
YOUR TAN

● Moisturise your face and neck morni
and night.

● Don't use bubble bath, bath salts or o
other bath product which might dry out
your skin.

● Add bath oil to your bath water or oi
your skin before bathing.

● After bathing, moisturise your skin wit
a good body lotion.

● If you have any extra cash, treat
yourself to some sunbed sessions!

s of autumn

**eaf through these ideas
nd make the most of autumn . . .**

ET'S MAKE-UP!

After the bright sunlight of summer,
tumn light is softer and more flattering
you can adapt your make-up to suit.
 autumn approaches the make-up
uses will bring out their new ranges of
umn make-up colours so take your time
d choose shades to suit your skin tone.
ere isn't a particular range which
peals to you then you can stick to the
ll-established earthy autumn colours
h as gold, brown and russet.

BACK TO SCHOOL . . .

● OK, so you're dreading going back for
yet ANOTHER term, but here's a few tips
to help you stay on top all through the
autumn . . .

● Splash out and buy yourself a whole
new set of notebooks and folders — it's
amazing how organised you'll feel, for a
little while anyway . . .

● Make sure you're always dressed
neatly. School shouldn't be an excuse for
a fashion parade but there's nothing
stopping you from looking smart and
fashionable! Choose a straight black or
grey skirt that'll look good with everything.
Opt for low black loafer shoes — they're
so comfy and look great with either ankle
socks or warm woolly tights. Splash out on
a big black cardie to keep you cosy all
through the winter and don't forget your
schoolbag — snap up a trendy satchel
type bag or steal your little brother's . . .

● If you're sitting exams, now's the time to
start swotting! Work out a reasonable
revising timetable — and stick to it! A few
hours every night (except weekends!)
should be enough to avoid that last minute
"I'll read my notes on the school bus" type
panic revision we all know about! Do the
same for homework too — leave yourself
enough time for each homework
assignment and cross it off in your
homework notebook as soon as you've
completed it.

SCHOOL LOOKS

● If you want to wear make-up to school
then keep the look as natural as possible.
There's no point plastering on powder
and paint when you know you'll just be
told to scrub it all off.
A light, tinted moisturiser should create the
ideal base. If you suffer from spots then
opt for a medicated brand or use a
medicated spot concealer. Make sure you
blend in well.
Give your cheeks some colour with a little
blusher and accentuate your eyes with a
couple of coats of a natural brown
mascara.
For the final touch give your lips a slick of
lip gloss.

ALL THE NICE GIRLS

What is it about a bloke in uniform that makes some girls go weak at the knees? Abby Butterick investigates . . .

YOU have to admit that there's something slightly different about a bloke in uniform. No, clever chops, we're not talking about bus conductors, postmen, traffic wardens or lollipop men — it's the ones in the Forces we mean!

When it comes to soldiers and sailors, rumours are rife. "A girl in every port," people say, shaking their head in disapproval. "Wild bunch. All wine, women and song."

So how do the uniform-clad male contingent measure up in reality? Three girls spill the beans about their experiences . . .

"You couldn't trust them an inch."

Lorraine is 18. She met Andy at school a year and a half ago, and was devastated when he announced that he'd been accepted for the Navy.

"It was just the fact that he was leaving and hadn't mentioned his plans at all. I'd got a place at college and I presumed he'd be going too — he's always wanted to be an engineer and he could easily have found a place on a course.

"We threw a party for him when he left, and I think I must have cried the whole way through. He'd been my first real boyfriend, you see, and I suppose I'd neglected my friends while we'd been together. I had absolutely no idea how I was going to cope without him.

"Andy promised to write, but deep down I didn't believe a word of it. Everyone in the Forces had girls all over the place and you couldn't trust them an inch.

"To my relief, Andy did write, and I began to feel a bit more hopeful about our relationship. Things were a bit strained when he came home on leave for the first time — he'd changed quite a bit — but we had a long chat and both decided we weren't really interested in anyone else.

"When he's with his Navy friends, Andy's a different person. They're a loud, showy crowd and I'm not particularly keen on them, but if I'm going to stick with Andy that's just something I'll have to put up with. He's still the same person underneath, after all.

"Sometimes I feel left out when my mates talk about boys they fancy, but I've no intention of seeing someone behind Andy's back. I can trust myself and I can trust Andy — and anyway, I happen to think he's well worth waiting for."

LOVE A SAILOR

"I couldn't see the attraction."

Kate is 17 and had been going out with Paul for two years when Mark arrived on the scene. "Our town's the kind of place where nothing ever happens, so when word got around that a whole load of sailors had arrived for a couple of days, everyone was determined to get to know them.

"My friends spent ages dolling themselves up all ready for a night on the town, and I kept thinking how stupid it all seemed. I couldn't see the attraction, to tell you the truth. I had Paul and that was all I cared about.

"We went along to the disco that evening, and I ran into a few mates there who were hopping about in excitement. For once the male/female ratio was more in our favour and talk about getting attention — the sailors were all over us! It was all very flattering considering that the local boys rarely give us a second glance.

"By this time, Paul wasn't too happy — the sailors were taking up practically the whole of the dance floor and one jostled him accidentally. It was Mark. Paul stormed off to moan about the sailors with his mates, and Mark stayed with me.

"I've never met anyone like him. We hit it off right from the start, and he seemed so much more exciting than Paul. He'd travelled so much and seen such a lot — and I suppose I was swept off my feet.

"That night I blurted out to Paul that I didn't want to see him any more. He flew into such a rage that he stormed off before I could explain anything, although I didn't really care at the time. Mark was all that mattered.

"We spent a fantastic couple of days together. When the time came for Mark to leave, we promised to write, phone and see each other as often as we could. The fact that Mark came from London and I live up north didn't seem to matter at all — after all, Mark had told me he loved me.

"I did write to Mark — every day to start with, because I could think of nothing else. But I didn't hear anything from him. Eventually a letter arrived — a very short, curt one that could have been written to anyone. It just said that I was a 'nice girl' and although he'd had a great time, he already had a steady girlfriend at home that he'd conveniently forgotten to mention. By that time, I realised exactly what I'd been missing and was desperate to get back with Paul,

but of course it was too late for that.

"Paul and I are friends again now, but that's all we'll ever be. I suppose I read far too much into something that Mark obviously thought of as a two-day fling."

"There's a certain excitement attached to the Forces."

Mandy is 16. "I can't resist a bloke in uniform! I met Gary, who's in the R.A.F., at a friend's party, and although we were only together for a couple of weeks before he was sent out to Malta, we had a brilliant time. Gary was tall, good looking, really popular and great fun to be with — he introduced me to lots of his friends, too, and we all got on really well.

"Obviously I was pretty upset when Gary left, but I'd known all along that he'd have to go so I'd tried to treat the whole thing in a really light-hearted way.

"It came as a bit of a shock, I thought, when a whole load of letters started arriving. There'd be at least a couple a week, and a little while ago Gary announced that he'd like to come to stay for a couple of weeks during his next leave.

"Whether it'll work out for us or not, I really don't know. To tell you the truth, I'm not sure whether it's Gary I'm so fond of or the whole image of it — there's a certain excitement attached to blokes in the Forces. I think it's those short haircuts I go for!

"I've been seeing a boy while Gary's been away, although it's nothing serious, so it'll be weird when we meet up again . . . I'll just have to see what happens. I still feel a bit too young to be tied down and I don't really want to get into anything I'm not sure about."

Well, here we are, all trying to look sane, sensible and normal. There's Cheryl on the end at the left with the blonde hair, she's 22 and is a hairdresser, but does loads of other things besides, like collecting clothes from the sixties. Martin's next to her, he's also 22 and is an actor. And next to Martin is *me!* I'm the Jackie fashion editor, and shan't bore you with the details. Beside me is Jalle, who's our fave make-up artist from Sweden who you probably recognise from some of our fashion pages (tends to get in the picture a lot).

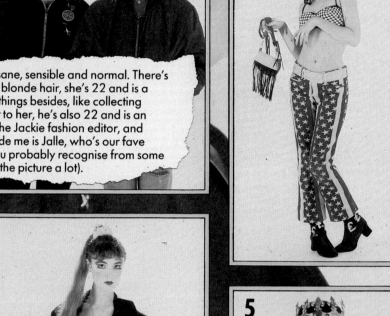

PIC 2. Cheryl's wearing Stars And Stripes jeans, her £ sign boots and an electric blue wig!

PIC 3. Martin shows a leg! Funny chap always did enjoy wearing his mother's frocks. All his clothes are from jumble sales . . . might have done with a shave, though!

PIC 4. And of course me, in my Miss Leatherette look. I've got on a Wet Look mac, a minisculish bikini and boots, they're all second hand. My Elvis rosette was bought for me by my dad.

PIC 5. The Handsome Prince. Jalle's feeling in a right royal mood, all crown jewels belong to his majesty . . .

PIC 6. Check out that pout! Martin steals the show . . .

PIC 7. Pretty in pink is Cheryl, with a lilac Afro wig.

PIC 8. Go west, young girl! An outfit I made together with Jalle's hat and wig.

PIC 9. Jalle's all zipped up with his punky scarecrow look.

PIC 10. All tarted up, with nowhere to go (mind you, who'd let us in?).

8.10 a.m.: This morning is not going well at all. First I wake up half an hour later than usual, then I can't find an un-laddered pair of tights and now Sigue Sigue are on the box and I *hate* them.
But to breakfast.
I usually start my day with a bowl of brose (which sounds a bit like what Oliver Twist asked for). I put a deep based pan on the ring with a cupful of water and waited till it boiled. Well, I usually do that — this time I forgot to switch the cooker on at the socket and it was a couple of minutes before I twigged. Anyway, once it boiled I sprinkled in two heaped dessertspoons of medium oats that I'd bought at the local healthfood shop. You've got to do it gradually or it all lumps together, so, stirring madly, I mixed the oats and left it to boil for about five minutes.
I used to cover my brose with heaps of sugar, but since I discovered honey I've been smothering mine in that!

8.30 a.m.: Cup of caff, methinks, before I dash out. I'm trying to cut out sugar altogether, but you know what it's like. I actually used to take *three* spoons, but I've got it down to a half, which is about nine calories or so.

8.45 a.m.: A quick walk down the road and I'll be in work a couple of minutes before nine. I work for an insurance firm, and it's quite a good laugh even though the work's quite hard.
I have the feeling, though, that I've left something at home . . .

8.50 a.m.: Like my packed lunch, for example! Oh, why can't I be more organised? I wasted five minutes going back to my bedsit to pick it up. Still, worth it — there were two pasties, a stuffed tuna egg, a crunchy salad and a bag of ready salted. I made the pasties a couple of nights before and these were the last of them.
To start, I bought a 7 oz. frozen pack of puff pastry and left it out to defrost, which took about an hour. Then I cut the rinds from four rashers of bacon and chopped the bacon up into smaller pieces. I added the bacon to one small chopped onion, half a pound of sausage meat and salt and pepper and (as they say in all the best cookery books) battered it to death in a bowl!
The next step was to grease — lightly — a baking sheet. Then I rolled out the pastry thinly and cut five 'rounds', using a saucer as a template. In each of the rounds of pastry I splodged a lump of sausage mix and brushed the edges of the pastry with water. That done, I crimped the edges together and put the pasties on the baking sheet, after basting them with egg. They usually take about 25 minutes in the oven of my bedsit's tiny cooker. That's at about 220°C (gas mark 7 on my mum's cooker, back home!).
The stuffed tuna eggs are dead easy — I make them quite a lot. It's just an egg, hardboiled for 12 minutes and then plunged into cold water till it's cold. Once it's cold I take the shell off, cut the egg lengthwise in half, scoop the yellow yolk out and mash it with a fork. I add a small dollop of salad cream, some salt and pepper and some tuna. Then I pipe the mixture back into the egg halves.
Tuna eggs go really well with salad, but I find it too much hassle to make a good crunchy salad, so I buy mine from Markies!

9.02 a.m.: In to the office at last, *with* my packed lunch firmly rammed under my arm. I was only slightly late and I don't think anyone noticed.

· COOK · COOK ·
COOKABILITY

9.15 a.m.: Well now, that was a surprise. Steve, the office charmer, actually spoke to me for about five minutes! I think it was so that I would be complimentary about his new grey suit (" . . . with blue flecks in it. Cost an arm and a leg, it did . . ."). Still, it makes a change from only exchanging nods in the lift at five o'clock.

11.10 a.m.: The girl who sits next to me has accused me of being obsessed by food. The cheek! Just because I told her, over our communal bag of canteen crisps, that whereas Golden Wonder contains 160 calories, Smith's Square crisps only 135. And it doesn't take a fool, I said, to work out that you can eat a fifth more square crisps. And it was as I was wiping the crumbs off my top lip that *he* returned. He sort of, well . . . draped himself over the desk and asked (seductively) if I'd be interested in lunch. Would I? Ha! Stuff the packed lunch! Shirley (the girl who sits next to me) was sick.

12.45 p.m.: I stood to look at my reflection in the mirror. My make-up wasn't too bad. A quick smudge with the concealer and I'd be ready to rejoin Steve 'Office Hunk' Smith back at the table. Perhaps I would have preferred something a little more romantic than a MacDonalds, but there we go.

12.55 p.m.: Disaster! There was I, just telling Steve that there are 555 calories in each Big Mac, that's without chips, of course, when I noticed a bit of bun had

fallen on his tie. I leaned over to flick it off and . . . knocked the MacDonalds Chocolate Thick Shake into his lap. His ne[w] grey suit (with the blue flecks) got almost a[ll] of the 390 sticky brown calories.
Steve's face turned from a pleasant pinky colour (with a rather cute dimple on his chi[n]) to a deep purpley red. He stood up and glared at me.
"Look . . . what you've . . . ohhh!" He looked at his suit. He looked at me. He go[t] redder still.

1.20 p.m.: I put the bag of wholemeal macaroni back on to the shelf. I didn't real[ly] need it after all. What's more there was a basketful of stuff I don't need to buy. Comfort buying, obviously. I mean there was a jar of lemon curd in there and I haven't eaten that since I was about six years old!
That must have been the shortest-living relationship I've ever had. I don't really thin[k] Steve will be that interested in seeing me again after all the things he called me. Clumsy cow, indeed. Huh!

1.55 p.m.: I finished telling Shirley about my tragic lunchtime and how I'd met Stev[e] as I came into the office and tried to apologise but he'd walked off. I'd even offered to have his stupid suit dry-cleaned but he was having none of it. Shirley looke[d] at me all wide-eyed as she filed her nails. "What a terrible shame." She tutted and shook her head. "Well, he'll be looking for someone else to take out , I suppose . . ." Bitch!

4.00 p.m.: Usually I get hungry around this time and have a bag of crisps, but I've kinda lost my appetite today.
Acksherly, crisps are really straightforward to make. All you need is a couple of good quality potatoes, peeled and then sliced very very thinly with a sharp knife. That's the difficult bit — that and trying to avoid slicing off any digits.
After there's a sizeable pile of potato slices you load them into a pan of hot fat with a basket. They take — if they're sliced thinly enough — about a minute to crisp.

5.15 p.m.: Typical. When it comes to going-home time the rain begins to belt down. Just after I left the office I popped into the local greengrocers to buy three satsumas. Satsumas never fail to cheer me up — they always remind me of Christmas, when dad used to wrap them up in silver paper and put them in my stocking. Those and walnuts that I could never crack the shell of to eat — to this day I still don't know what they taste like!

6.05 p.m.: Well, it looks like my diet (diet? What diet?) has gone completely to rack and ruin. I sought solace in the last three peanut butter cookies that I made on one of my baking sprees about a week ago.

8.30 p.m.: As I think I said before, today is not going well. I've just scalded my hand while trying to drain some spaghetti. It's the steam, I'm forever doing it! The spaghetti's for my tea. It's later than usual, but then the telly was uncommonly good tonight.
After finally dragging myself from the box I decided to make my very own version of spaghetti bolognese. The sauce is another one of my bung-it-in-a-pan-and-see recipes. The basic ingredient is a tin of chopped tomatoes, which is dead cheap, to it you add tomato puree (a splodge of), salt and pepper, Italian seasoning and fried, chopped rashers of bacon (four of) or a small tin of ham or pork, or something, chopped small.
As I say, you just bring it to the boil and simmer it for twenty minutes or so.

10.30 p.m.: Before I go to bed I'll bake some more peanut butter cookies since I finished the last lot off tonight.
Like all of the things I cook or bake it's a really easy recipe.
I took 2 oz. of smooth peanut butter, 2 oz. of normal butter (although I sometimes use marg.), 2 oz. of caster sugar and 1½ oz. of soft brown sugar, the rind of an orange (grated off) and smoothed it together in a big bowl.
To that, I added half of a beaten egg, 1 oz. of chopped raisins and 4 oz. of self-raising flour, sieved. Then I mixed it all together to make a firm-ish dough.
I divided it up into ten lumps and rolled them out into small balls before flattening them onto an ungreased baking sheet.
I baked them for 25 minutes at 180°C until they were golden, then set them out on to a wire try to cool.
The room smelled brilliant!

11.30 p.m.: Lights off. Sleep-byes time.

11.32 p.m.: Lights on again! I forgot to wind the clock up — I don't want tomorrow morning to be a repeat of this morning. Tomorrow! Will Steve ever look at me again? Worra fiasco that was . . . probably should have seen it coming. As my mum says, I *always* make a meal of things . . .!

THE WAY WE WERE

What the rich and famous did before hitting the big time!

Teacher:
Tom Bailey (Thompson Twins)
Sheena Easton
Sting
Dionne Warwick
Bryan Ferry

Shop Assistant:
Steve Bronski (Bronski Beat)
Pete Burns (Dead or Alive)
Dave Gahan
Boy George
Tony Hadley (Spandau Ballet)
George Michael
Anne Nightingale
Jimi Somerville (The Communards)
John Taylor

Advertising:
Tony Hadley

Factory Worker:
Howard Jones
Stuart Adamson (Big Country)
Marc Almond
Mike Nolan (Bucks Fizz)
Paul Young

DJ:
Mikey Craig (Culture Club)
Nick Rhodes
George Michael

Accountant:
Stuart Adamson

Actor:
Divine
Leee John (Imagination)
Gary Kemp (Spandau Ballet)
Martin Kemp (Spandau Ballet)
Simon Le Bon

Joe Leeway (Thompson Twins)
Toyah

Catering:
Holly Johnson (FGTH)
Madonna
Jon Moss (Culture Club)
Jimi Somerville
Larry Steintachek (Bronski Beat)
Mick Talbot (Style Council)

Labourer:
Gary Daly (China Crisis)
Dave Gahan (Depeche Mode)
Green (Scritti Politti)
Shirlie Holliman (Wham!)
Paul Humphreys (O.M.D.)
Bobby G. (Bucks Fizz)
George Michael
Mike Read
Holly Johnson
Sting
Rod Stewart

Graphic Designer:
Adam Ant
Nick Heyward
David Bowie

Lifeguard:
Madonna (!)

Dancer:
Jay Aston
Tracey Ullman
Toyah

TV Delivery Man:
Feargal Sharkey

Hospital Staff:
Morten Harket (a-ha)
Mags (a-ha)

wake

FESTIVE FLAB!

● It's really easy to pile on the flab in winter, so, before it's too late and someone mistakes you for a snowman follow our tips for keeping in trim . . .

● If you must have Christmas pudding take just a small piece and have it with natural yoghurt instead of lashings of brandy sauce or cream.

● It's better to eat half a mince pie with 55½ calories than a whole one with 111

● If you get lots of chocs for Christmas don't be tempted to guzzle them all at once. Treat yourself to a couple of sweets then give the rest to your mum or save them to give as birthday presents — that way you'll lose weight but save money!

● Once you've had your Christmas meal, instead of lounging about in front of the telly go for a walk and get some fresh air. If it's been snowing, build a snowman or have a snowball fight!

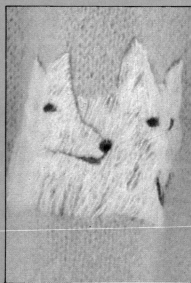

up to winter

Hot stuff for cold days . . .

SAVE YOUR SKIN

Always protect your skin against harsh winds and biting cold — use a moisturiser, a salve and hand cream every day. Be specially careful if you go skiing and make sure you use a high protection suntan product to protect your skin from the harmful rays of the sun.

PAAARTY!

● Follow our top tips for a perfect party!

1. Plan your guests carefully. Don't stick to inviting couples or just everyone from your class — they'll all know each other and that's not much fun, is it? Invite a few friends from home and school and balance the guest list between boys and girls!

2. Avoid gatecrashers! If you shout about the party at every opportunity, everywhere you go you're asking for trouble! And ask your friends not to bring along anyone you don't know very well!

3. Don't worry about food and drink too much! Make up a fruit juice punch and stick big bowls of crisps all over the room! If you fancy something a bit more exotic, why not try baked potatoes with different fillings or cut up crusty bread and serve with paté.

4. Spend a few days before your party making up tapes of all your favourite records. You'll never be able to suit everyone's tastes but stick to good dance or chart singles that'll get most folk on their feet. A record player is OK but be prepared for a pile of scratched records the next day . . .

5. Don't spend a fortune on invitations — make your own. Cut up brightly-coloured card into twendy shapes and write all the relevant information clearly on the front ie. time, place, date etc. It's a good idea to stick R.S.V.P. on it too, so you'll know exactly who's coming!

6. Use plastic plates and cups for your grub and you'll have lots less trouble clearing up after the party. Grab an enormous black bin bag and lug everything in, give the place a quick run over with the vacuum cleaner, replace the furniture if you've moved anything and you'll never know there's been a party.

MAKE YOUR OWN CHRISTMAS CARD

● All it'll cost you is the card, the paint/ ink/blood, or whatever you're going to draw or print with, and the envelopes. One of the simplest but classiest ways to make your own cards is to make 'splatter' cards: Get your large sheet of card, a pot of poster paint and an old toothbrush. Dilute the paint slightly and dip the brush in. Then flick the paint across the card, for biggish splashes of colour, or run the edge of a knife up the stubble of the brush to create a spray effect.
Experiment with different colours of backing paper and paint until you find colours that go together well.
Once the card has been 'splattered' cut it into envelope sized 'cards'.
Et voila . . .

DROP 'EM

Nothing comes between a boy and his underpants — except our guide to who wears what . . .

UNDER COVER

The Y-front

Yuk — Y's are pretty bad anyway but if they're the patterned nylon kind then you might as well give him up as a dead loss. These are the sort of things that people like Ken Barlow would wear. I mean, could you imagine the Pet Shop Boys in patterned Y-fronts?

The Posing Pouch

A string of elastic and a strip of satin the size of a postage stamp are all that goes into making these. He's likely to be a bit of a show off and likes to think of himself as a macho-man. More than likely to be a club DJ or a football player.

Motifs and messages

We are talking wally with a capital W! Can you believe there are actually boys around who still wear those horrid nylon things with saucy messages on them? The fella inside these probably has a mental age of about 3½.

Boxer Shorts

Per-witty twendy chap you've got here, especially if they're crisp white ones like the fella in the Levi's ad! Blokes with boxers are so twendy they probably wear 501's anyway. All the top pop people wear them and even if they are bright red polka dot ones they do put him head and shoulders above the crowd! You'll need to try hard to keep up with the guy in boxers!

3 in a pack

His mum buys them from Markies for him, in variations of stripes and contrasting colour bands. Generally worn by the dependable boy-next-door type, who wants to settle down with a nice little girl-next-door. He's the type you'll end up marrying—and who knows, maybe in a few years time he'll send YOU out to buy them.

Doesn't Wear Any

Well, well, well — what can we say!!!?

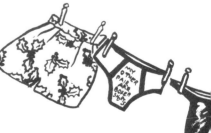

COLOURS

Black

Smoochy, sexy character with a dark side to his personality which is best kept hidden. Not a lot of fun but definitely a bit of a mystery.

Blue

A calm, relaxed person who takes things day by day and won't go for the "love at first sight" job. More likely to ask you out after he's known you for about ten years.

Green

Nature lover — his idea of a perfect date is a walk in the forest followed by a quick snog behind the bushes. He's also a great talker, tending to get very excited at the least little thing — i.e. spotted woodthrushes.

Yellow

A colour chosen by boys with a sense of adventure who won't wait for things to come to them. They'll go for it with a typical unconventional approach.

Red

A leader of the pack. Strong and full of himself — likes to be the centre of attention. If you're happy to play second fiddle, then that's fine, but if not, steer clear of the guy in the red briefs!

White

Likes the simple things in life, but if the truth be known, he's also a little bit of a poser. The healthy, sporty type who only comes out in the summer months.

MORE *dash* THAN CASH

THE piggy bank has surrendered its last penny. Your coat pockets have nothing to declare but a couple of bus tickets, an old paper tissue and a fossilised chunk of Yorkie. When an advance on next week's pocket money is all that's keeping the wolf from the door, it's about time you got yourself organised . . .

If you can't rustle up the entrance fee to The Hippodrome this Saturday, don't despair. There's lots going on for free!
● Youth clubs aren't just ping-pong and prawn-flavoured crisps, y'know. If yours isn't up to scratch, get together with a couple of friends and change it!
● Youth theatres, dramatic clubs and dance workshops are often short of members — who knows, you could end up ballroom dancing champion of Clacton-on-Sea.
● Museums, libraries and art galleries are for the more sedate — keep your eyes peeled for intense young men with paint-stained fingers, boffins and budding poets!

● Evening classes are not only for those who long to learn Cantonese. If you can't find a class you like, then round up some mates and invent your own.
● Voluntary Work is really satisfying and it can be good fun. You can do just about anything, from shovelling snow for the elderly to clearing out canals.
● The Duke of Edinburgh Award Scheme is a way to combine lots of different activities — you need determination and hard work to collect your award, but it's well worth it.

To find out more about what's available in your area, contact the Citizens' Advice Bureau, the local library, the Volunteers' Bureau or just look in the Yellow Pages under "Clubs and Associations — Leisure & Cultural". Many sports centres, cinemas and theatres offer reduced admission for the unwaged, too, so don't be too scared to ask.

Chauffeur-driven Rolls off the road for a while? Fret not. There are alternatives . . .
● Bicycles are a girl's best friend — if you haven't got one already, flash the second-hand section of the newspaper under your parents' noses and remind them of the bus fares you'll save.
● British Rail have a Rail Riders card (if you're under 15) or a Young Persons Railcard (for 15-24 years olds) which save on fares.
● If you're over 14 and in full-time education, get hold of an International Student Identity Card from your local Student Travel Service, or by writing to: National Union of Students, PO Box 190, London WC1. This will get you cut-price travel and loads of other discounts.
● Walk! Go on, it'll do you good . . .

MONEY: You'll manage to fritter away your money if you don't exert a little self-control. It would be a good idea to save a little for an unexpected expense towards the end of the year.

HOLIDAYS: Your sparkling personality will attract interest from people you meet on holiday. They'll all think you're great fun — be careful not to be too overpowering. They might be a bit put off!

FRIENDS: You're used to having a little clique of friends around you. Why not look outside this little group sometimes? It'll stop you having too narrow a view of life.

WORK/SCHOOL: This year you're going to have to put your mind to your work a bit more. You're usually so busy with other things that you can't find time to fit in that homework.

HIGH POINTS: Other people will appreciate your loving, generous nature and you'll benefit by gaining new friends. 1987 will be best remembered for new friendships.

LOW POINTS: At times you're too pushy and domineering and people might not realise that you have feelings just like anyone else. Don't worry though, you'll not be down for long!

VIRGO
AUGUST 22-SEPTEMBER 21

LOVE: You're not what you'd call backward at coming forward, are you? This is a major characteristic of your starsign and should see you having an eventful if not always happy lovelife this year.

MONEY: You're not the sort of person who likes to be flash with your cash but you do like to treat yourself now and then. Virgo girls hate lending money, but if you do weaken then make sure that you're paid back in full!

HOLIDAYS: If you can't afford a holiday abroad, try going for day trips to different places. Your stars suggest that you'll be meeting lots of new people and this could be your ideal opportunity.

FRIENDS: When you feel down, you tend to be critical of others, try and forget about your own worries. This sort of thing can lose you friends. Try not to take your bad moods out on them.

WORK/SCHOOL: Another characteristic of your star sign is your love of books. As long as you keep away from the Jackie Collins and stick to Maths Made Easy you should do all right this year.

HIGH POINTS: Your love life is either going to be your highest high or your lowest low. If you're careful and don't rush into things then 1987 could be a year for romance that you'll remember for a long, long time to come. Your sense of humour should brighten things up for others.

LOW POINTS: Your temper could be your downfall this year, so watch your step. Keep your mind on your schoolwork as bad exam results could seriously affect your future.

LIBRA
SEPTEMBER 22-OCTOBER 22

LOVE: Your love-life may seem a bit boring at the start of the year but by April things should be really taking off! If you've been involved in a long-term romance you may have to decide whether this is what you really want. Don't worry, though — whatever you decide, love is well-starred for the rest of '87.

MONEY: Saving money is usually one of your strong points but don't spoil your fun by saving for a rainy day. Splashing out occasionally on yourself or your friends won't break the bank!

HOLIDAY: Holidays are high spots in your life and you love looking through piles of brochures dreaming of exotic locations. Don't spend all your time dreaming, though — make up your mind where you'd like to go and go for it!

FRIENDS: You may find that 1987 is a year for forming new friendships. Your old pals may begin to drift away, either to pursue various careers or various boyfriends! Don't feel lonely, though — make an effort to make new friends and keep in touch with old ones!

WORK/SCHOOL: 1987 calls for a lot of hard work but it'll be worth it in the end. Don't be tempted to give up if things don't seem to be going your way — stick in there!

HIGH POINTS: The summer of '87 should be the high spot of your year with holidays and love well-starred. Don't let the sun go to your head though — keep your feet on the ground!

LOW POINTS: 1987 may start off slowly for you but try not to let it get you down — better things are on the way . . .

SCORPIO
OCTOBER 23-NOVEMBER 21

LOVE: This will probably be an active year as far as the old love life is concerned! What you'll have to avoid is expecting too much from your boyfriends. Don't lean so heavily — you'll only scare them off.

MONEY: We're talking broke here, unless you keep your spending in check. There may be an opportunity to make money at the start of the year, but you'll need to be quick.

HOLIDAYS: Start making plans now, or you'll be left with nowhere to go and no-one to go with. Any you do go on, though, will be brilliant!

FRIENDS: When all around are losing theirs, you'll remain friends with pretty much everyone. However, watch that your oldest friend isn't feeling left out.

WORK/SCHOOL: There'll be a lot of changes as far as this is concerned. Watch that people in authority don't see you as being conceited.

HIGH POINTS: Your family life will be surprisingly good and you'll meet a lot of interesting, enthusiastic people.

LOW POINTS: Let's face it, financially you're a loser! Money will be your biggest problem over the year.

SAGITTARIUS
NOVEMBER 22-DECEMBER 21

LOVE: This year looks like being good in love for all Sagittarians. You won't be short of admirers, but try not to be too casual with your relationships, or you might end up hurting someone.

MONEY: You'd expect Sagittarians, with their lively, careless natures, to be fairly useless with money, but oddly enough you're quite reliable. Don't be frightened to treat yourself now and again, though.

HOLIDAYS: Sagittarians aren't known for their quiet, passive natures, and lazing around all day on a Spanish beach probably isn't your idea of fun (can't think why not . . .). You're more likely to enjoy more active holidays — hill-walking, for instance.

FRIENDS: One thing you don't need to worry about in 1987 is friends! You're fun to be with and always seem to know when someone needs a shoulder to cry on.